Alfred's
Premier Piano Course

Dennis Alexander • Gayle Kowalchyk • E. L. Lancaster • Victoria McArthur • Martha Mier

D1824013

Theory Book 1B is designed to correlate with Lesson and Performance Books 1B of *Alfred's Premier Piano Course*. When used together, they offer a fully integrated and unparalleled comprehensive approach to piano instruction.

In addition to written theory, unique features of the book include:

- *Fun Zone*—Explore music through written games and puzzles that truly make theory fun!

- *Imagination Station*—Learn to compose and create.

- *Learning Link*—Discover facts related to history, science, and interesting subjects from daily life based on the music and activities in the course.

- *Now Hear This*—Learn how to listen to music through ear training. Most of these exercises should be done in the lesson.

- *Now Play This*—Learn to sight-read music.

The pages in this book are correlated page by page with the material in Lesson Book 1B. They should be assigned according to the instructions in the upper right corner of each page of this book. They may be assigned as review material at any time after the student has passed the designated Lesson Book page.

Edited by Morton Manus

Cover Design by Ted Engelbart
Interior Design by Tom Gerou
Illustrations by Jimmy Holder
Music Engraving by Linda Lusk

Alfred

Just turn the page to start your exploration of the fascinating world of music theory!

Fun Zone **Cats and Dogs Everywhere!**

Trace (and shade if necessary) the music symbol
on each cat or dog.

1. **Minim**

3. Each bar gets 4 counts.
Each ♩ gets 1 count.

2. **Mezzo forte**
Play moderately loud.

4. **Semibreve**

5. **Semibreve rest**

6. **Dotted minim**

9. **Forte**
Play loudly.

8. Each bar gets 3 counts.
Each ♩ gets 1 count.

7. **Piano**
Play softly.

10. **Minim rest**

Fun Zone

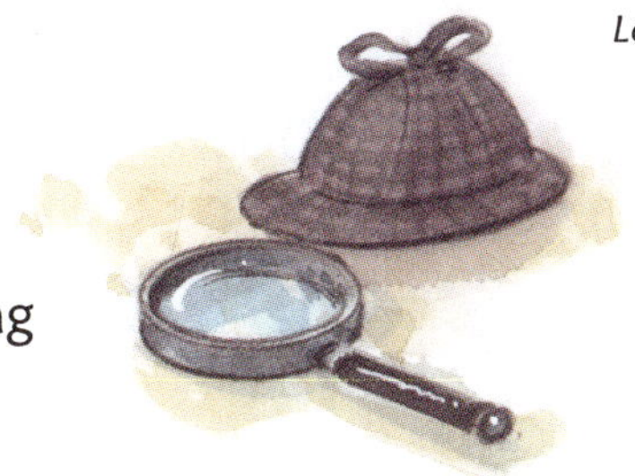

1. Musical Detective: Be a musical detective by answering the questions about the music. Then play and count aloud.

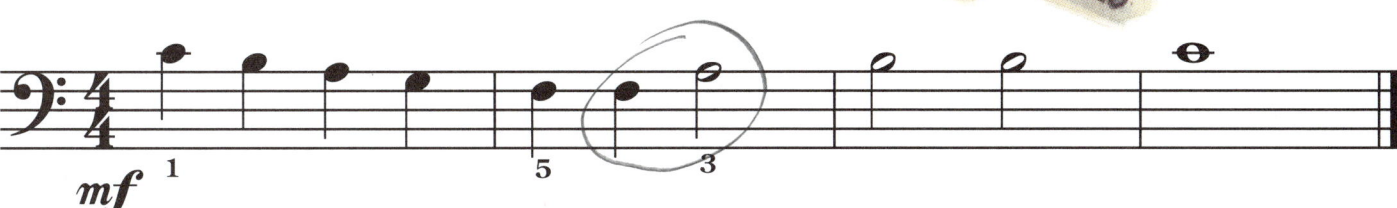

a. Which hand plays the piece? _left_

b. What finger plays the first note? _Thumb_

c. How many beats in each bar? _4_

d. The note F repeats in bar 2.
What note repeats in bar 3? _B_

e. Find the skip and circle it.
What are the two notes that skip? _F A_

2. Note-Name Match: Draw a line from each note to its letter name.

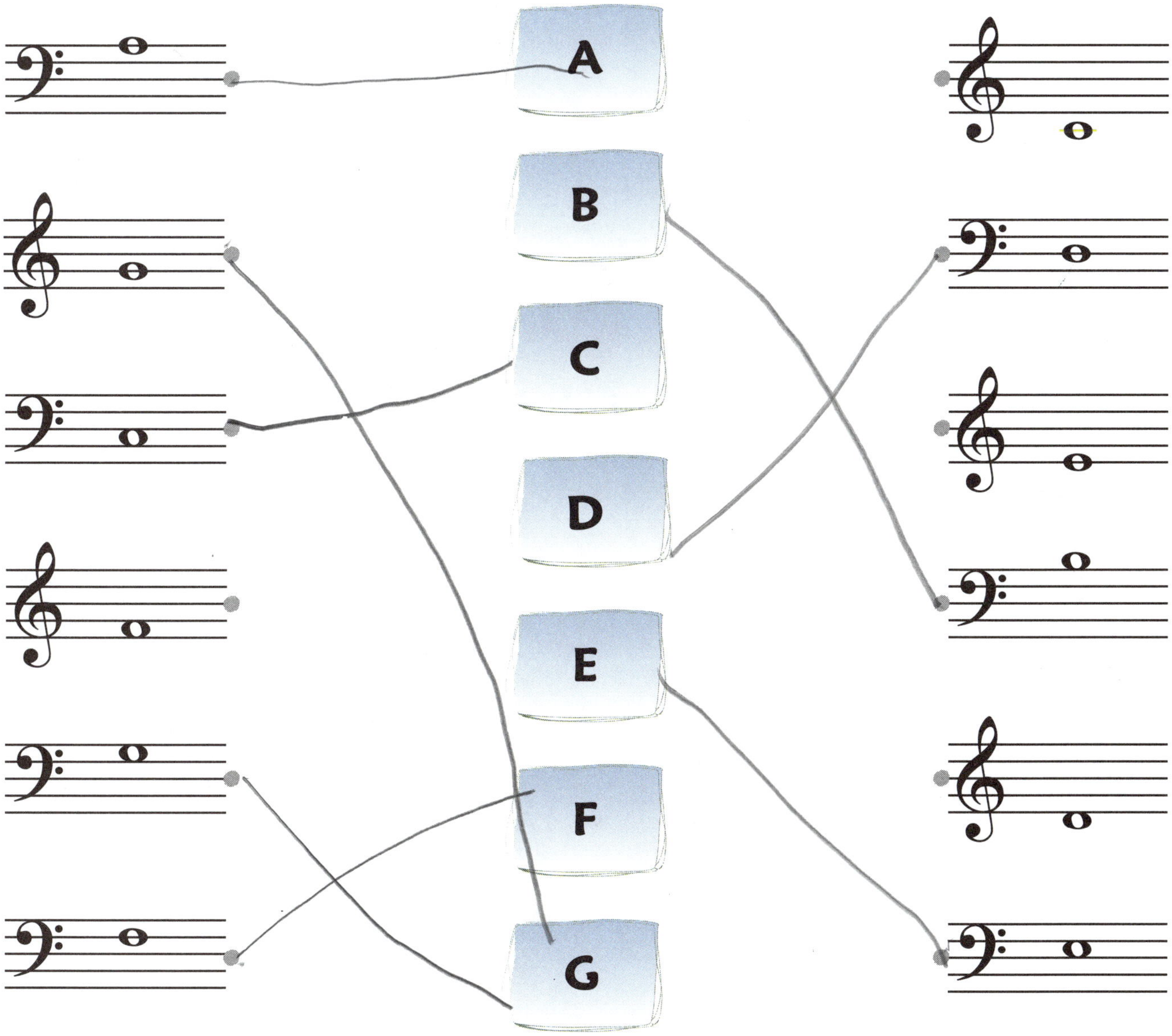

A

B

C

D

E

F

G

Rhythm and Time Signature Review

1. Write the answer on the line:

    a. How many crotchets in each bar of $\frac{3}{4}$ time? _____

    b. How many crotchets in each bar of $\frac{4}{4}$ time? _____

2. Write the correct time signature ($\frac{4}{4}$ or $\frac{3}{4}$) for each rhythm pattern.
   Then tap and count aloud.

a.    **b.**

c.    **d.**

3. Tap and say the words.

a.

    Sing   a   new   song.

b.

    Sing   this   song.

c.

    Sing   songs.

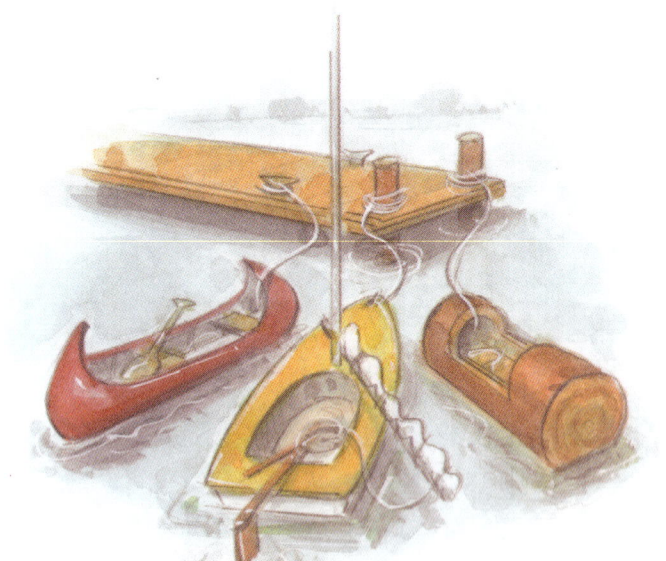

Imagination Station

*Make up new words to fit the rhythm pattern.
Write them below the notes.*

Your
words:

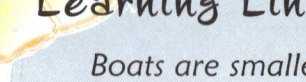

Learning Link

Boats are smaller than ships. The first boats were canoes made from hollowed-out logs. Today, many boats are used for pleasure and recreation. Some are powered by motors; others use sails; a few use oars. They are often stored in marinas where they are tied to **boat docks.**

Steps or Skips

1. **Now Hear This:** Your teacher will play steps or skips.*
   Circle the pattern that you hear. Then circle *steps* or *skips.*

2. **Now Play This:** Before you play, write the name of the first note and say *step* or *skip* as you point to the notes that follow. Then sing (or say) the letter names as you play.

Note to Teacher: Play one pattern from each exercise.

Fun Zone **A Visit to Yosemite**

Fill in the blanks with note names to spell words about sights in Yosemite National Park.

Learning Link

Yosemite National Park, *located in central California, is a great wilderness. It is a spectacular area of mountains and valleys that includes numerous trails, beautiful lakes, rushing streams, waterfalls, mountain peaks and giant Sequoia trees. Many kinds of animals and birds live there. A number of rock masses rise from the valley floor, including the famous Half Dome and El Capitan—both favourites of experienced rock climbers.*

1. V __ L L __ Y

2. __ __ __ R

3. __ __ __ R

4. L __ K __

5. W O O __ __ H U __ K

6. __ __ __ L __

7. __ __ __ L L S

1. **Now Play This:** Play the rhythm pattern, using the correct hand, note and finger. Count aloud.

Steps or Skips

2. Write the name of the key that is a *step* or *skip* (up or down) from each labelled key.

Example

3. Write a minim that is a *step* or *skip* (up or down) from each note. Then play.

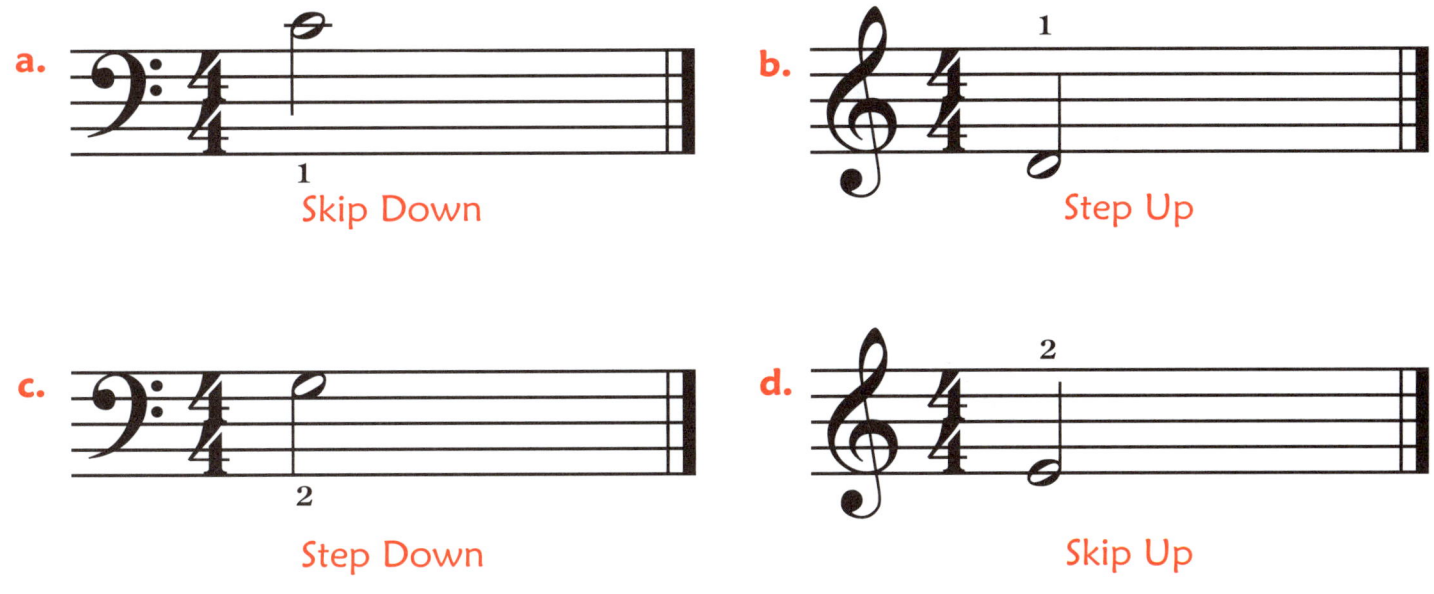

a. Skip Down

b. Step Up

c. Step Down

d. Skip Up

8

Tie

1. Draw an X through each example that is *not* a tie.
   Remember: Ties connect notes on the same line or space.

   a.   b.   c.   d.

2. In each example, draw a tie to connect the two notes that are on the same line or space.
   Remember: stems *down*—ties go *over* noteheads; stems *up*—ties go *under* noteheads.

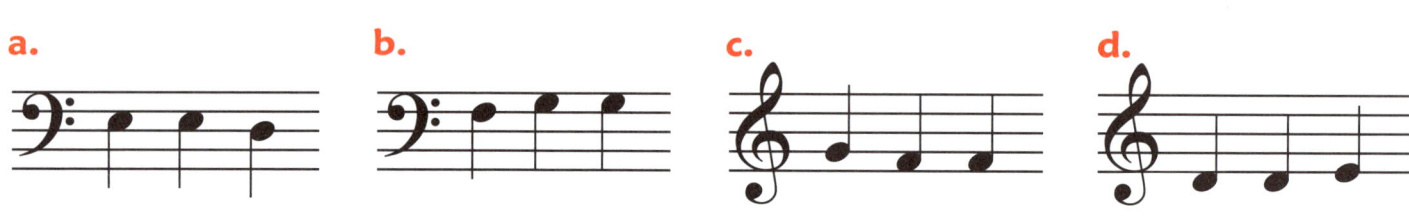

   a.   b.   c.   d.

Learning Link

Approximately 70% of the world lies underwater. **Snorkelling** is a great way to see fish and coral under the sea. Colourful coral reefs can be found in the warm waters of most oceans. Australia's Great Barrier Reef contains some of the world's most beautiful coral reefs.

3. **Rhythm Addition:** Add the counts for the tied notes (𝅘𝅥 = 1 count).

   a.   = _____ counts   b.   = _____ counts

   c.   = _____ counts   d.   = _____ counts

 **Fun Zone** **Time to Get Up!**

Add bar lines in the correct places in the examples below.
Then add the total beats to find the time the children get up on Saturday morning.
Write the counts under the notes.   Then tap and count aloud.

1. 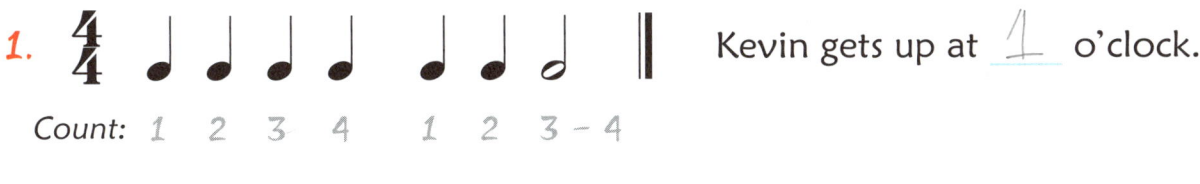 Kevin gets up at 1 o'clock.

Count: 1 2 3 4   1 2 3 – 4

2.  Emily gets up at 10 o'clock.

Count:

3. Jason gets up at ____ o'clock.

Count:

4.  Michelle gets up at ____ o'clock.

Count:

5. Antonio gets up at ____ o'clock.

Count:

6. Add one or more notes to this rhythm to show
   what time you get up on Saturday morning.

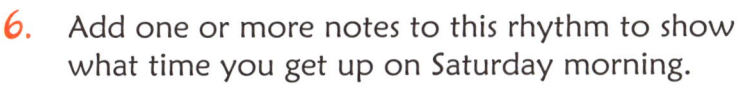 I get up at ____ o'clock.

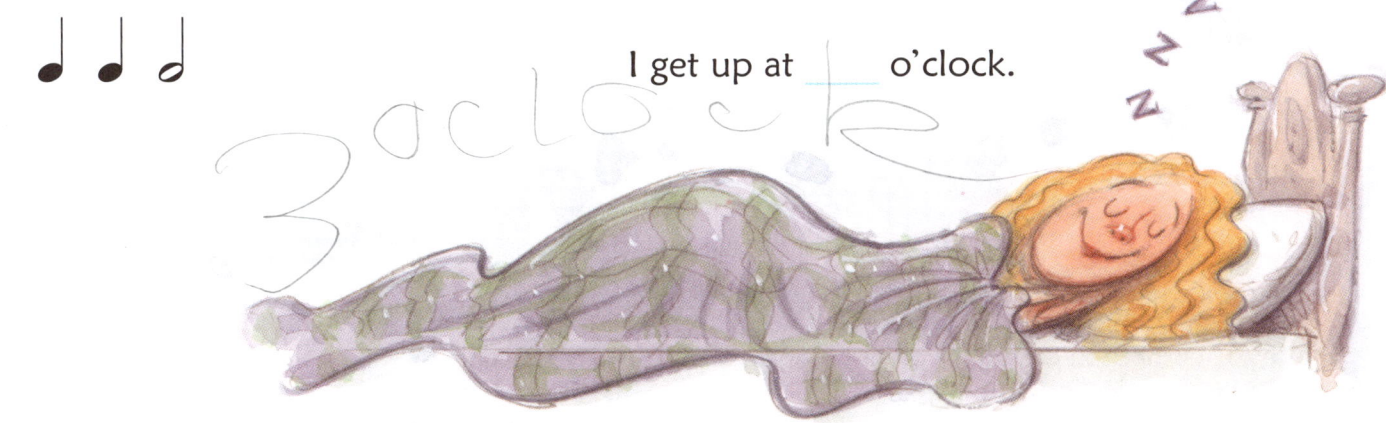

Steps and Skips

1. Circle each skip, then draw lines to connect the circles.

The circles will form a **square** **triangle** if you connect them correctly.

(circle one)

2. **Now Play This:** Play and count aloud. Watch for ties.

3. **Now Hear This:** Your teacher will play a step or skip *going up.**
Circle *step* or *skip*.

a.   Step
         Skip

b.   Step
         Skip

c.   Step
         Skip

d.   Step
         Skip

***Note to Teacher:** In the middle of the keyboard, play a step or skip up.

A in Treble Clef

1. A *step up* from Treble G is A. Using minims, write this A three times. Add a bar line and a double bar. Then draw a tie under the last two notes.

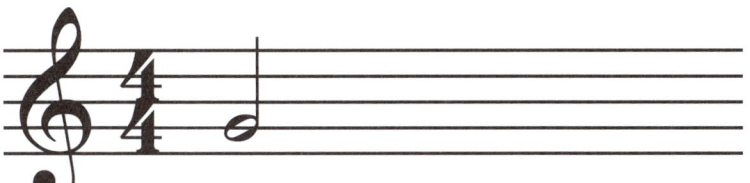

2. Write a minim that is a *step* or *skip* (up or down) from each note. Then name and play the notes.

a. Step Up

b. Step Down

c. Skip Down

d. Skip Up

3. Play each pattern of steps and skips. Then write the name of the last note.

LH
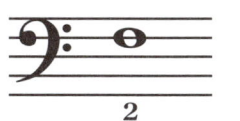
step   skip   skip _____

RH

skip   step   skip _____

Fun Zone **Rhythm Review**

1. **Ice Cream Cones** Draw a line from each flavour to its correct time signature on the cone. Say the flavours in the correct rhythm.

Learning Link

No one really knows when the first **cone** *was combined with* **ice cream.** *Some say it can be traced back to England in the 1700s. In the United States, a patent was issued in 1904 for one type of cone. This ice cream and cone combination first became popular at the 1904 St. Louis World's Fair. The Fair included about 50 ice cream stands and a large number of waffle shops. It did not take long for them to get together to produce a refreshing snack that is now popular throughout the world.*

mint choc-'late chip

rock - y road

cof - fee al - mond fudge

pep - per - mint stick

choc - 'late

Ne - a - pol - i - tan

2. **The Mystery of the Un-named Notes:** Read the clue for each note. Then draw the note, write how many counts it gets in 4/4 and/or 3/4 time, and name it.

Clues	Draw the note.	How many counts?	Circle its name.
● This note is oval-shaped, white inside, and has a stem.		_____	semibreve minim
● This note has a black oval and a stem.		_____	minim crotchet
● This note is oval-shaped, white inside, and has a stem and a dot.		_____	dotted minim crotchet
● This note is oval-shaped and white inside.		_____	minim semibreve

1. **Now Play This:** Play and count aloud.

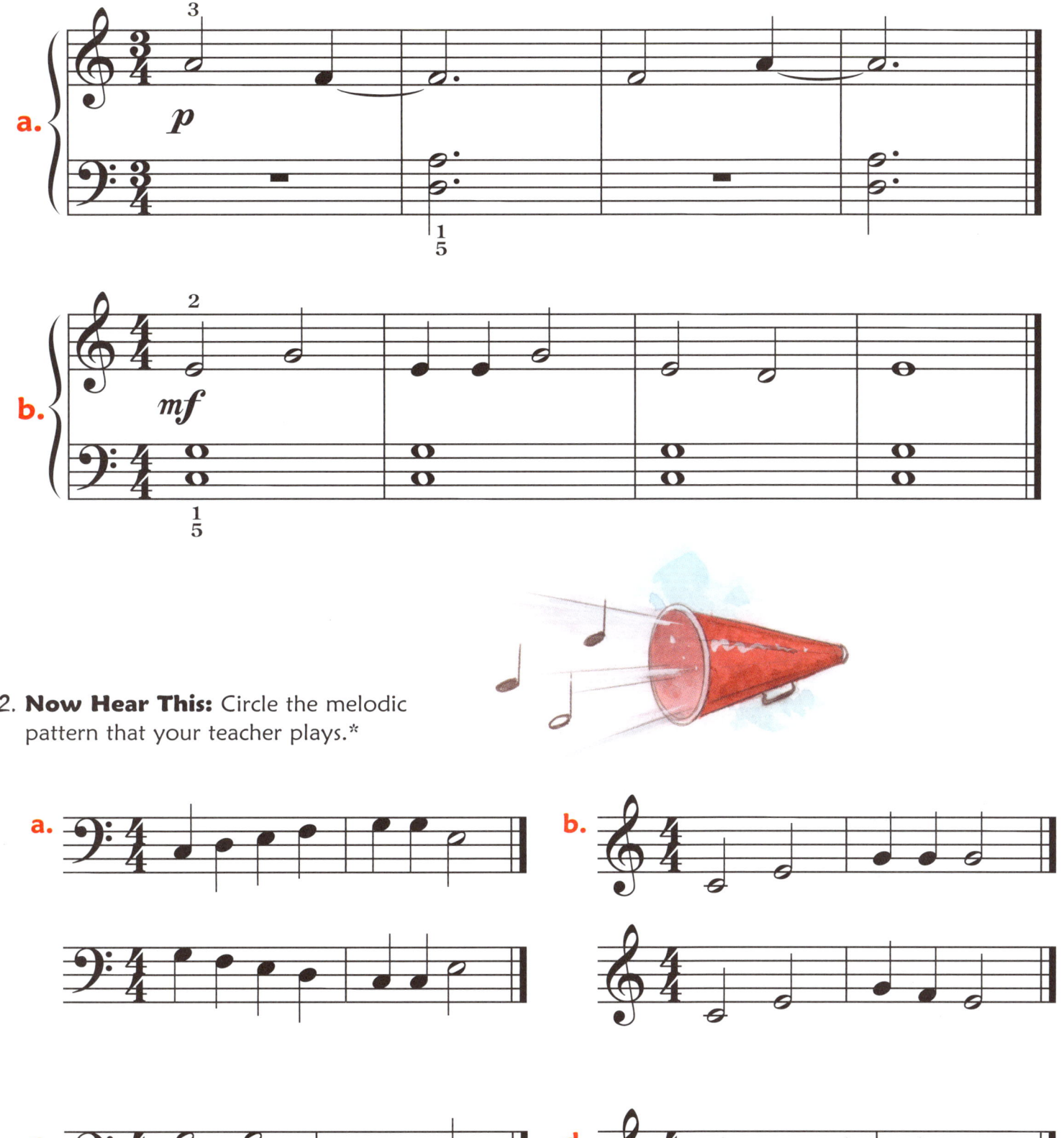

2. **Now Hear This:** Circle the melodic
pattern that your teacher plays.*

*Note to Teacher: Play one pattern from each exercise.

Legato—Slur

1. Trace the dotted lines to complete each slur. Then write the note names on the blank lines.

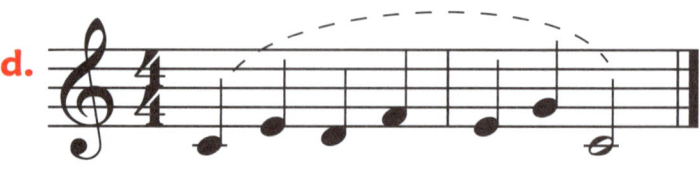

2. **Now Play This:** Complete the two slurs for each melody. Add a different dynamic sign (*f*, *p* or *mf*) in each box. Then play and count aloud. Remember to play *legato*.

3. Circle *slur* or *tie* for each example.

a.

Slur   Tie

b.

Slur   Tie

c.

Slur   Tie

d.

Slur   Tie

e.

Slur   Tie

f.

Slur   Tie

Staccato

1. Draw staccato dots for each crotchet. Then play and count aloud.
   Reminder: Dots go *below* notes with stems up, *above* notes with stems down.

2. **Now Play This:** Write *legato* or *staccato* on each blank line.
   Then play and count aloud.

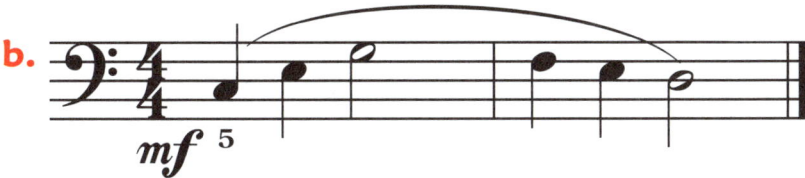

Imagination Station

A famous composer has chosen titles for some new music. Decide if each title describes music that is played staccato or legato. Then draw a line from the title to the correct word.

Floating Clouds		Jumping Kangaroo
	Staccato	
Pogo Stick		Flowing River
	Legato	
Ping-Pong		Graceful Dancers

Learning Link

Potato chips were invented by a cook named George Crum in 1853 in Saratoga Springs, New York. He took thin slices of potatoes, wrapped them in a cloth napkin, and dropped them in a tub of boiling water to cook. When they were done, he added salt. He later opened his own restaurant, and people came from near and far for his new "Saratoga chips."

1. **Now Hear This:** Your teacher will play five-finger patterns.* Circle *staccato* or *legato.*

a. Staccato
Legato

b. Staccato
Legato

c. Staccato
Legato

d. Staccato
Legato

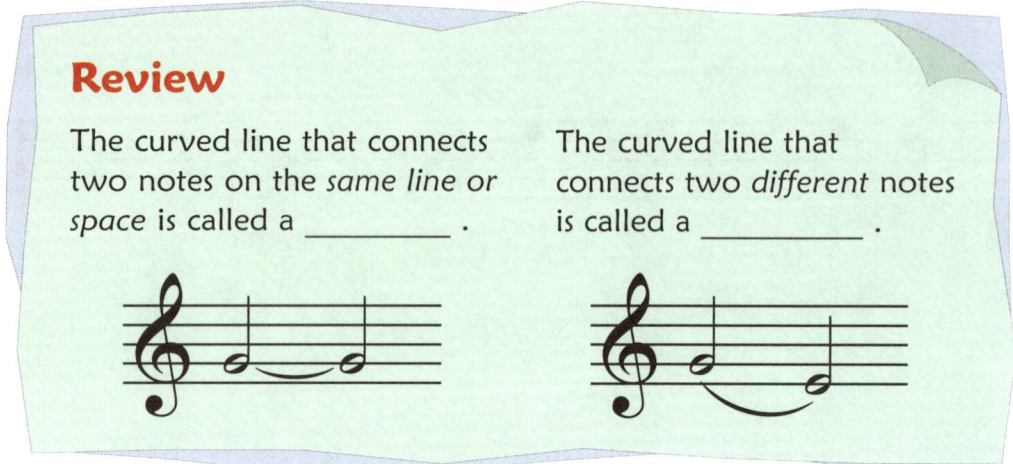

Review

The curved line that connects two notes on the *same line or space* is called a _____ .

The curved line that connects two *different* notes is called a _____ .

Fun Zone **Musical Detective**

2. Be a musical detective by answering the questions about the music. Then play and count aloud.

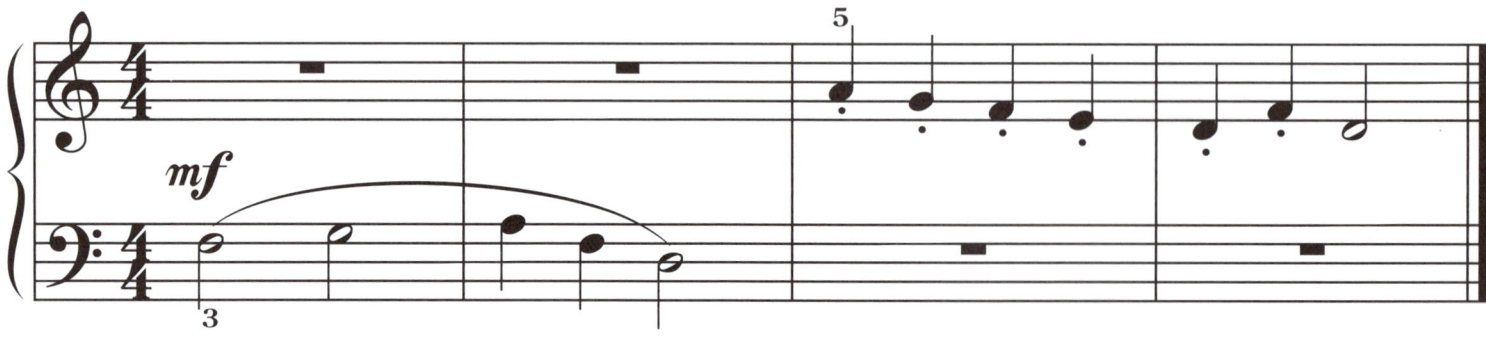

a. What is the name of the first note in the RH? _____

b. Does bar 2 have steps or skips? _____

c. Does bar 3 have steps or skips? _____

d. Which hand plays *legato*? _____

e. Which hand plays *staccato*? _____

Note to Teacher: Play *staccato* or *legato* five-finger patterns starting on any key in the middle of the keyboard.

New Rhythm Pattern

1. In the blank bars, write the new rhythm using the note that is *up a step* from Treble G.

New Rhythm on Treble G

Name note ____

2. Complete the new rhythm on Bass F.

3. Write the new rhythm using the note that is *down a step* from Bass F.

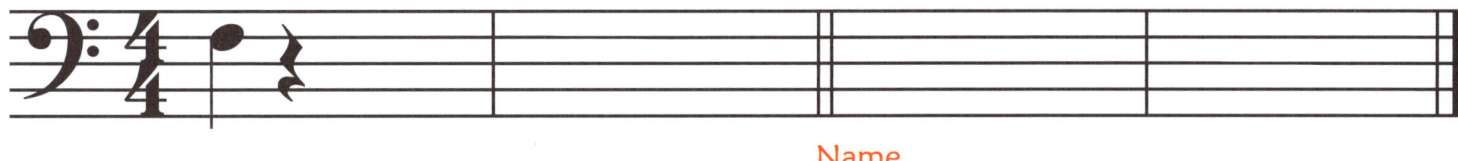

Name note ____

4. Draw a line from each word to its matching notes.

FEED

BAG

ADD

CAFE

2nds

1. Write the musical alphabet letter that is *up* a 2nd.

 a. **C** D   **b.** **A**   **c.** **G**   **d.** **E**

2. Write the musical alphabet letter that is *down* a 2nd.

 a. **B**   **b.** **D**   **c.** **F**   **d.** **A**

3. Write the names of the keys that are a 2nd *up* and a 2nd *down* from each labelled key.

Example

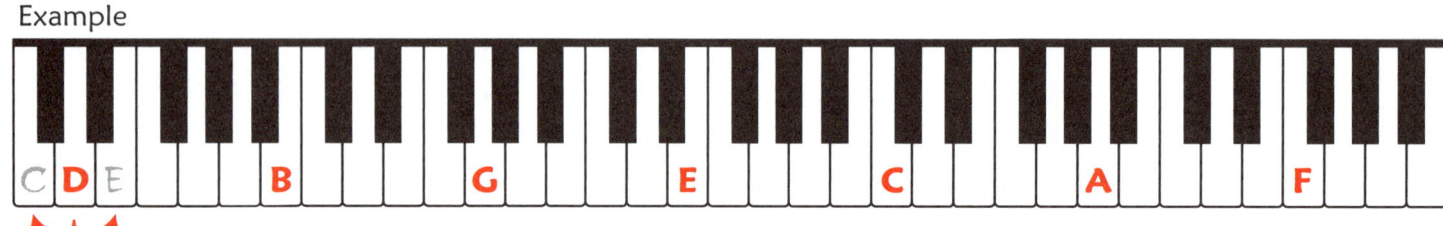

Down Up

4. Write a minim that is a *melodic 2nd* up or down. Then name and play each note.
 Remember: Stems *down* if notehead is *on* line 3 or above.
       Stems *up* if notehead is *below* line 3.

2nd Up   2nd Down   2nd Up

2nd Down   2nd Up   2nd Down

3rds

1. Write the musical alphabet letter that is *up* a 3rd.

   a.   E   **b.**   **c.**   **d.**

    C ˣ   **B** ˣ   **F** ˣ   **A** ˣ

2. Write the musical alphabet letter that is *down* a 3rd.

   a.   **G** ₓ   **b.**   **F** ₓ   **c.**   **B** ₓ   **d.**   **D** ₓ

3. Write the names of the keys that are a 3rd *up* and a 3rd *down* from each labelled key.

   Example

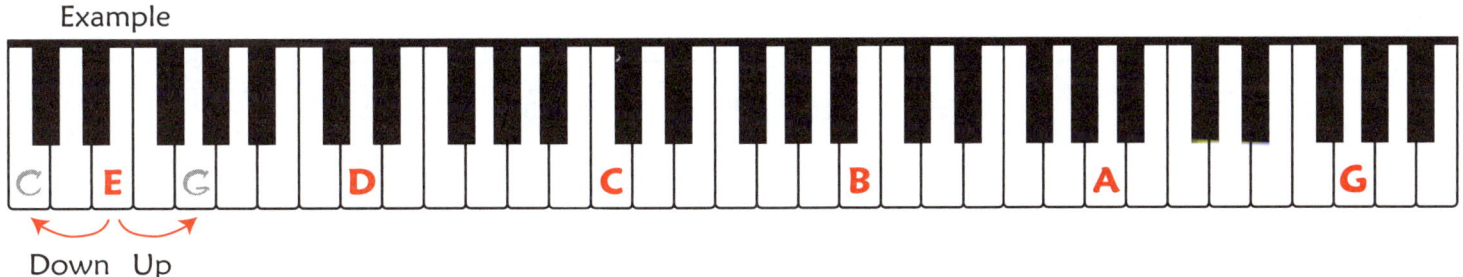

   Down Up

4. Write a minim that is a *melodic 3rd* up or down. Then name and play each note.
   Remember: Stems *down* if notehead is *on* line 3 or above.
                 Stems *up* if notehead is *below* line 3.

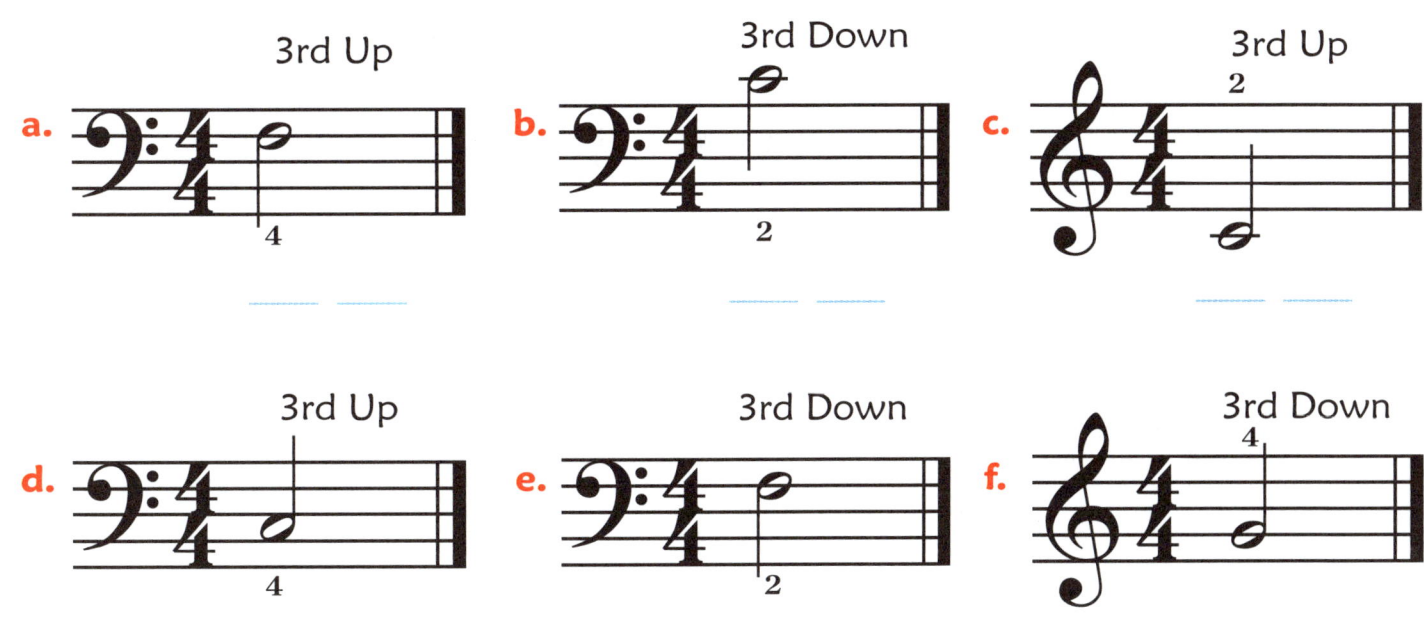

2nds or 3rds

1. **Now Hear This:** For each exercise, your teacher will play a 2nd or 3rd going up.*
   Circle the keyboard with the names of the notes that are played.

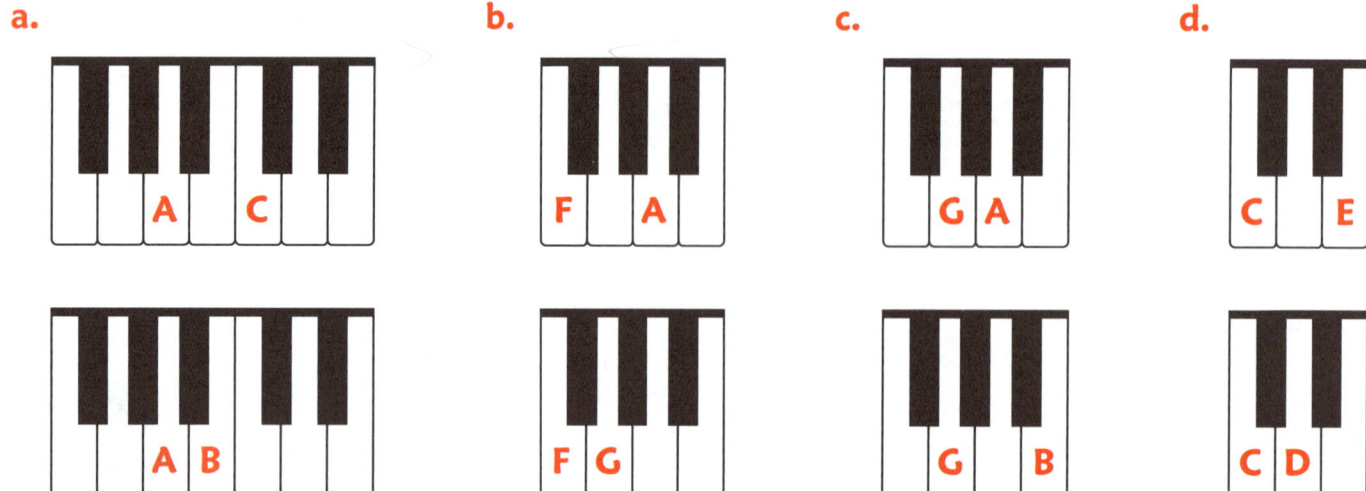

2. Write the interval name on the line. Then circle H for harmonic or M for melodic.

Learning Link

Popcorn *is a popular snack that had its beginnings in the United States. Indians in North and South America grew popcorn for more than 1,000 years before the first European settlers arrived. They popped it on hot stoves over a campfire and used it for food, decoration and in religious ceremonies. The centre of the popcorn kernel is soft and turns inside out when it pops.*

*Note to Teacher: Choose one keyboard from each exercise and play the melodic interval moving up.

Middle C, Treble C and Bass C

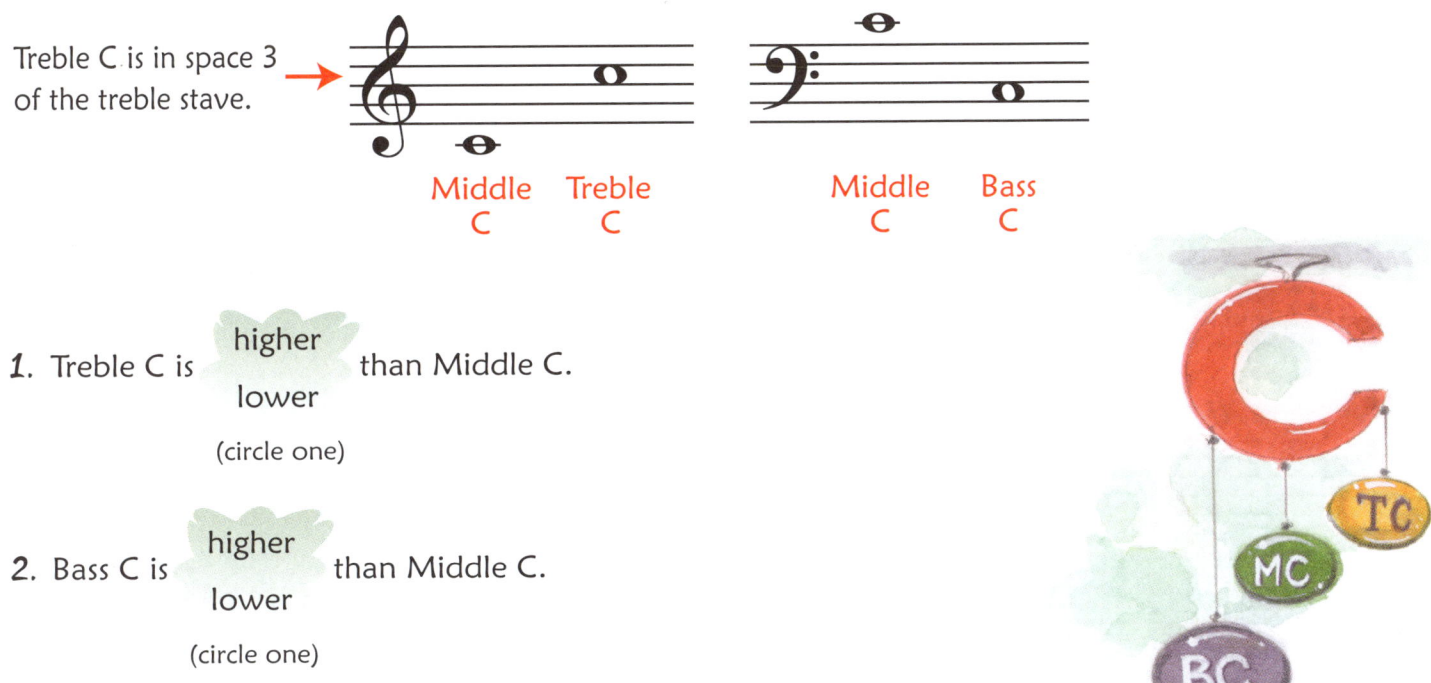

Treble C is in space 3 of the treble stave. →

Middle C   Treble C   Middle C   Bass C

1. Treble C is higher / lower than Middle C.

(circle one)

2. Bass C is higher / lower than Middle C.

(circle one)

3. Write TC for each Treble C, MC for each Middle C, and BC for each Bass C.

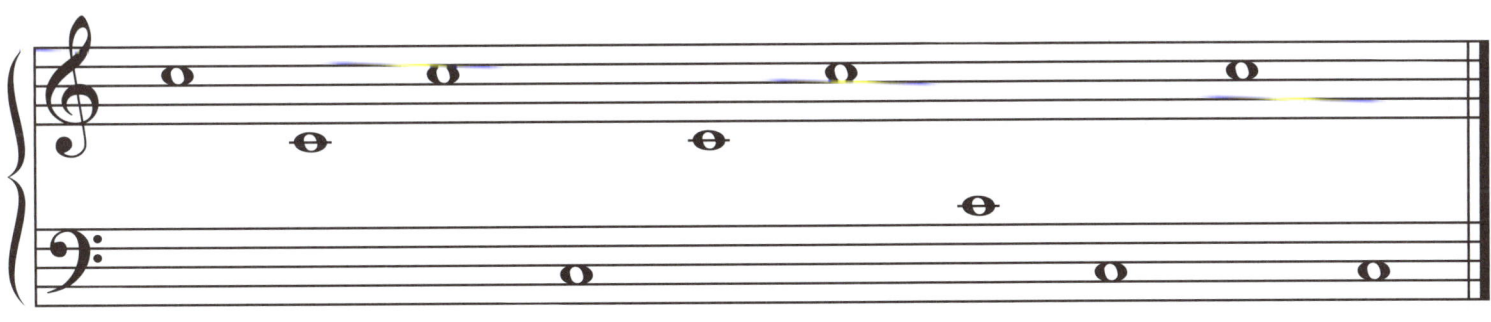

4. For the right hand, write the finger number that you would use to play *up* a 2nd from the given fingering.

a.   3 / 2   **b.**   4   **c.**   3   **d.**   1

5. For the left hand, write the finger number that you would use to play *down* a 2nd from the given fingering.

a.   1   **b.**   3   **c.**   4   **d.**   2

Fun Zone An Underwater Adventure

Name the notes to read the story.

___ R I ___   ___ OV ___   INTO TH ___   ___ OOL,

___ LU ___   W ___ T ___ R.   ___ IRST, H ___

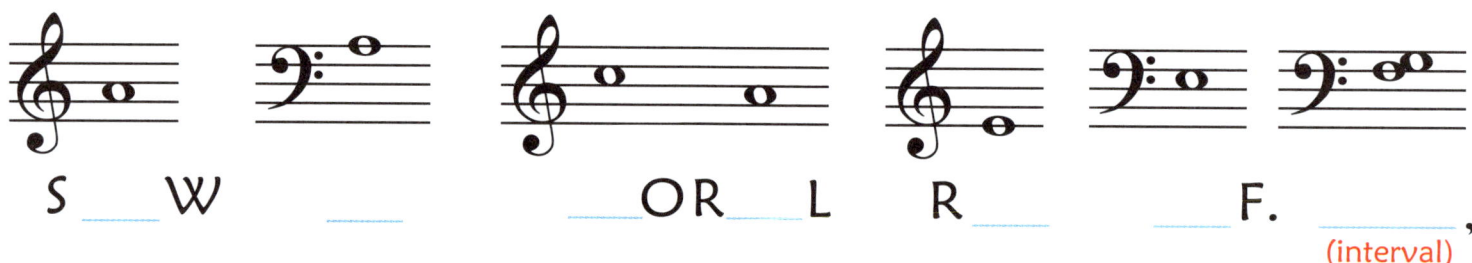

S ___ W ___   ___ OR L ___ R   F. ___ ,
(interval)

H ___   SW ___ M   BY R ___   ___ N ___   OL ___

___ ISH.   TH ___   ___ SI ___ HT   W ___ S
(interval)

___ HU ___   S ___   TURTL ___ !

New Notes B and D

1. Connect the notes to the matching letters.

C D B

D C B

B C D

B D C

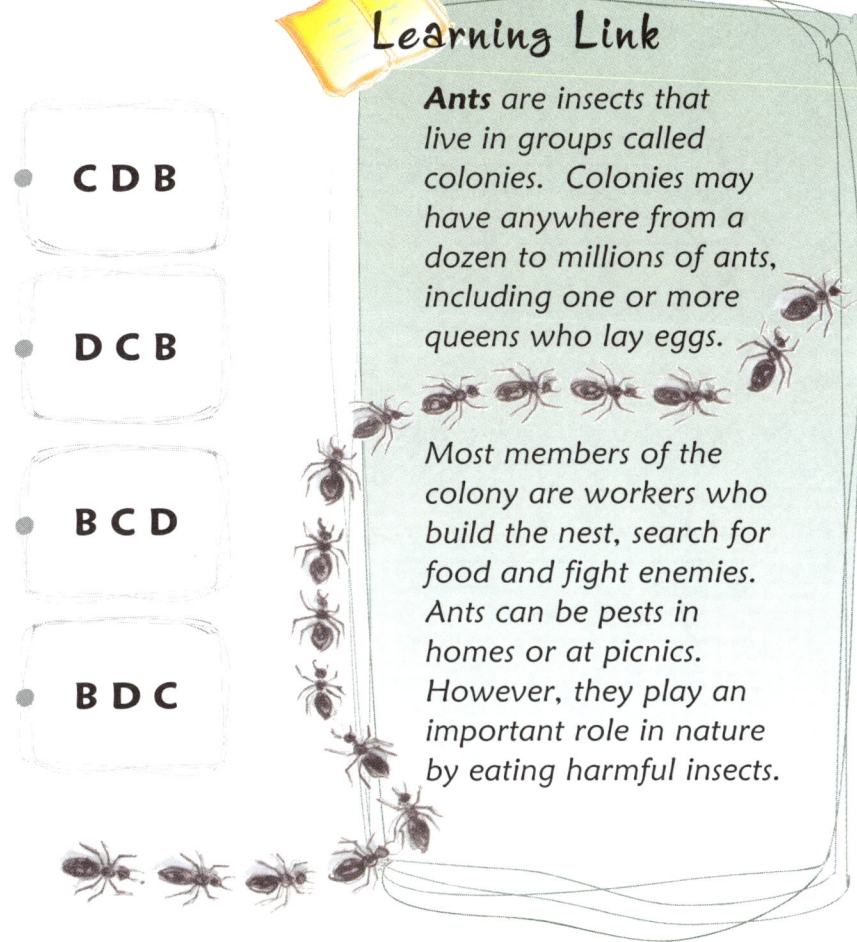

Learning Link

Ants are insects that live in groups called colonies. Colonies may have anywhere from a dozen to millions of ants, including one or more queens who lay eggs.

Most members of the colony are workers who build the nest, search for food and fight enemies. Ants can be pests in homes or at picnics. However, they play an important role in nature by eating harmful insects.

2. Draw a ✓ under all the 2nds on the staves and keyboards. Draw an X under all the 3rds.

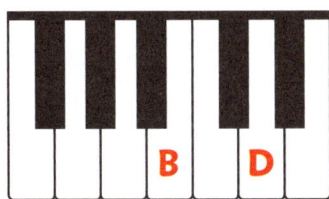

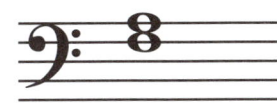
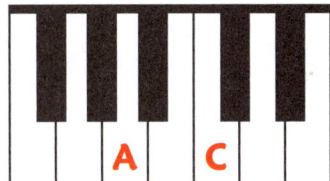

G 5-Finger Pattern in Treble Clef

1. Using semibreves, write the G 5-finger pattern *going up.* Name each note.

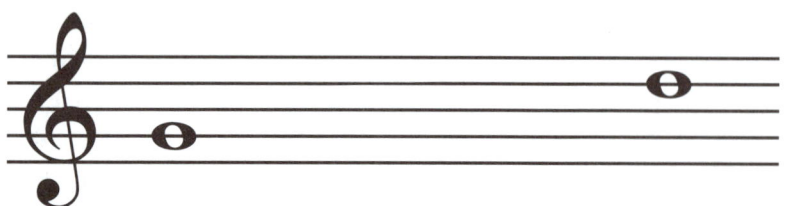

2. Using a semibreve, write one note that will make a 3rd between each note. Name the notes.

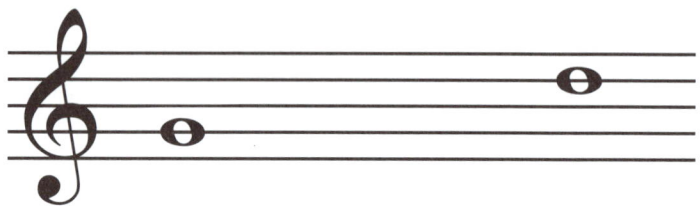

Learning Link

Butterflies live in all parts of the world. Many kinds of butterflies are found in tropical rainforests. Butterflies begin their lives as small eggs that hatch into caterpillars. After each caterpillar reaches full size, it grows a protective shell. When the shell breaks open, the caterpillar becomes a beautiful butterfly.

3. Name each note. Then circle *2nd* or *3rd.*

a. 2nd 3rd
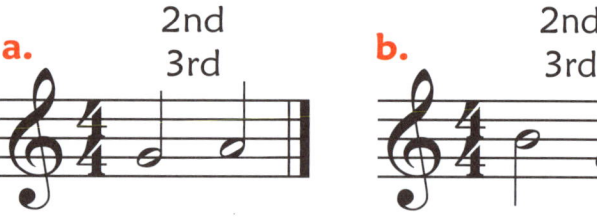

b. 2nd 3rd
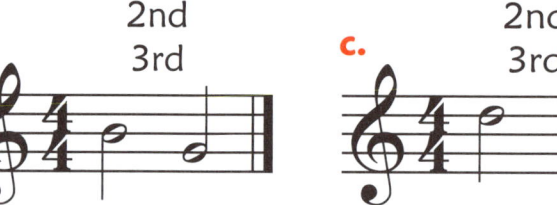

c. 2nd 3rd

d. 2nd 3rd

e. 2nd 3rd

f. 2nd 3rd

g. 2nd 3rd

h. 2nd 3rd

Imagination Station

Add one note under each arrow to complete the melody with notes chosen from the G 5-finger pattern. Write your choices on the stave and then play.
Remember: Stems down if notehead is on *line 3* or above.
Stems up if notehead is *below line 3.*

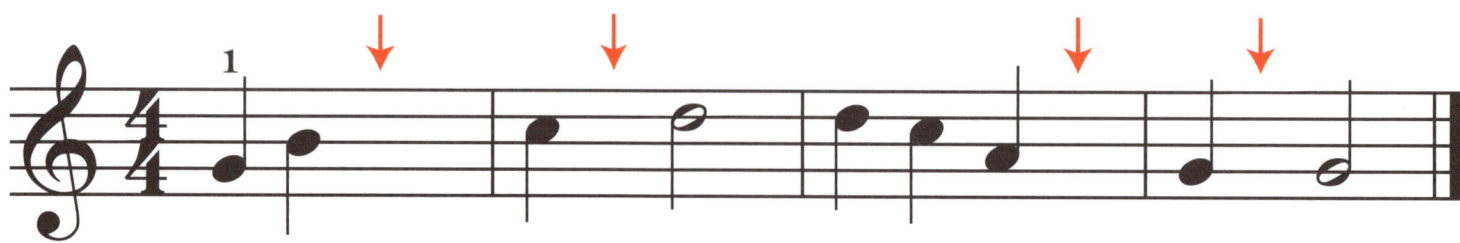

Bass G, Low G and Treble G

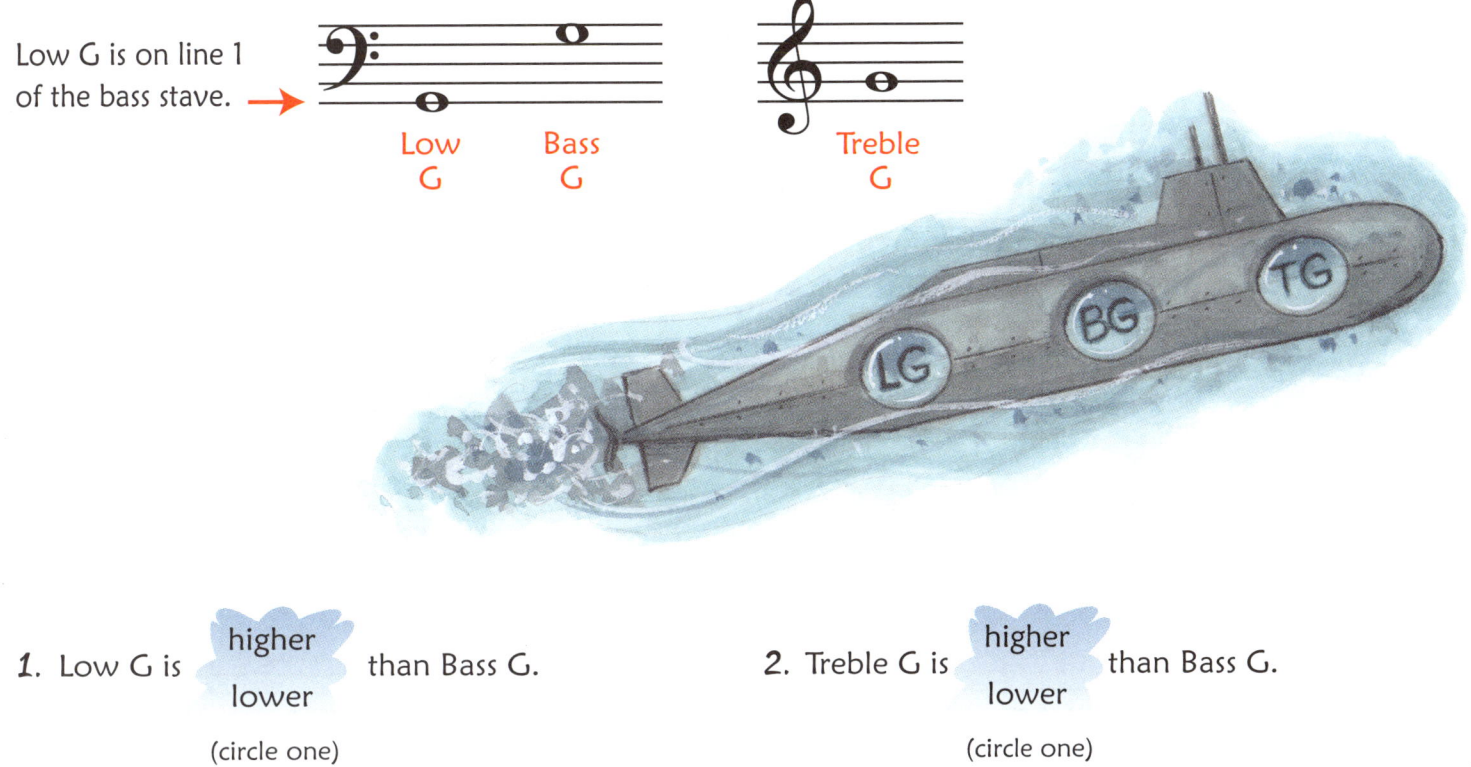

Low G is on line 1 of the bass stave. →

Low
G

Bass
G

Treble
G

1. Low G is **higher** / **lower** than Bass G.

(circle one)

2. Treble G is **higher** / **lower** than Bass G.

(circle one)

3. Write LG for each Low G, BG for each Bass G, and TG for each Treble G.

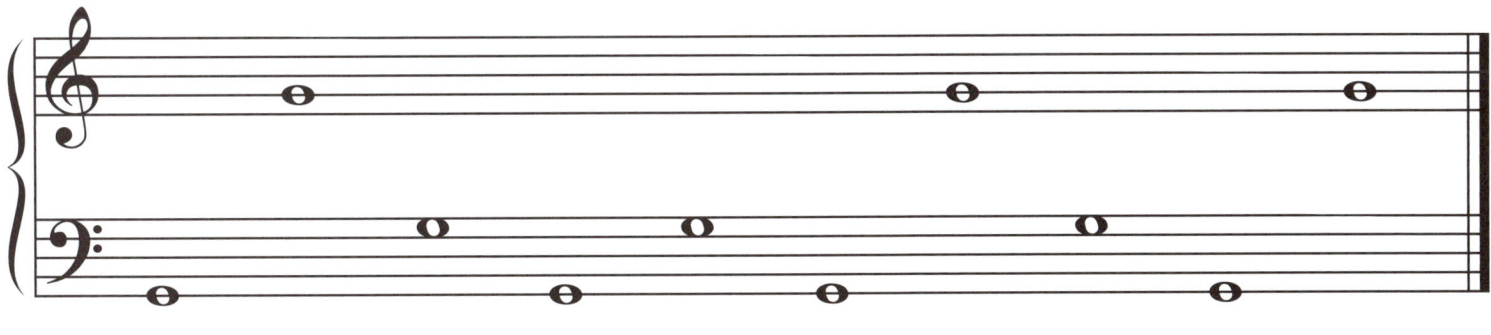

4. For the right hand, write the finger number that you would use to play *down* a 3rd from the given fingering.

a. 5   *3*

b. 4   ___

c. 3   ___

5. For the left hand, write the finger number that you would use to play *up* a 3rd from the given fingering.

a. 3   ___

b. 4   ___

c. 5   ___

Phrase

A phrase is similar to a sentence in language.
Each word (and note) is smoothly connected to those before and after.

1. Trace the phrase mark (slur). Then play and count aloud.

2. **Now Play This:** Read the words aloud. Complete each phrase mark
connecting the first and last notes of each phrase. Then play and count aloud.

a.
Ham - bur - gers,   hot - dogs   are   my   fav - 'rite   foods!

b.
Lon - don   Bridge   is   fall - ing   down.

c.
Will   you   come   and   play   with   me?

3. Play each phrase below, making each note smooth and connected. Count aloud.

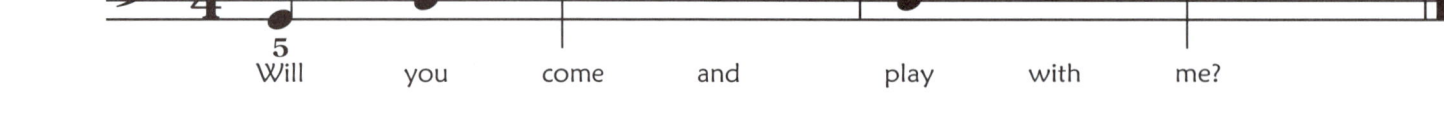

a.
I'm   a   phrase;   con - nect   my   notes!

b.
Hear   the   phras - es,   smooth - ly   played.

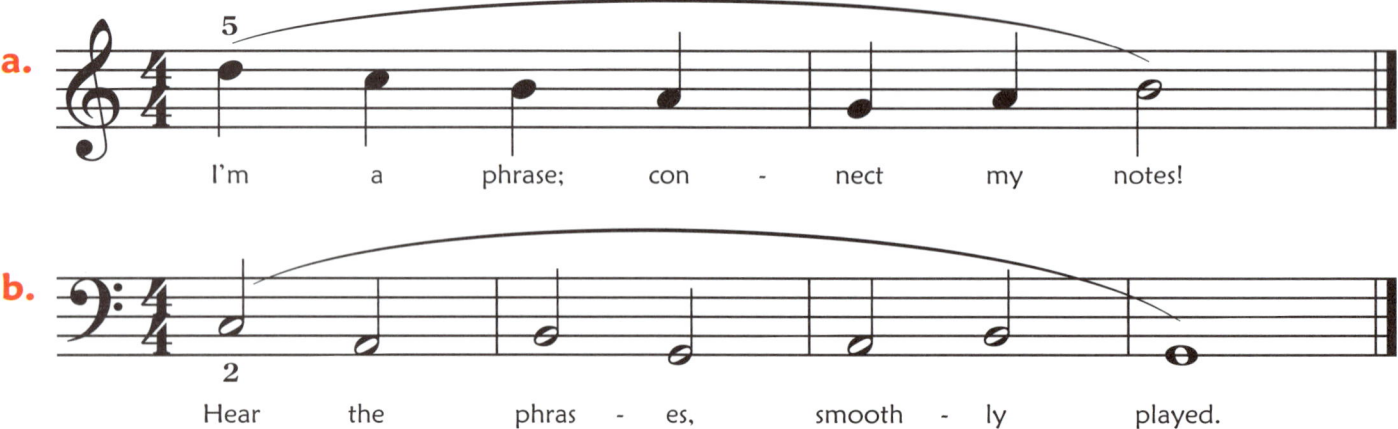

Fun Zone Noteworthy Crossword

1. Fill in the crossword puzzle by writing the names of the notes in the squares.

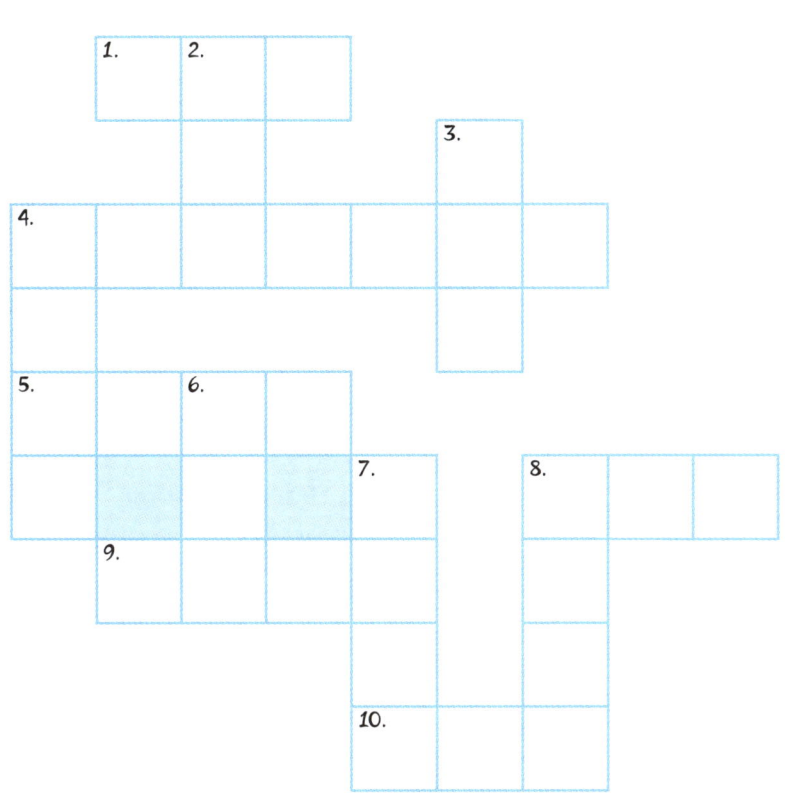

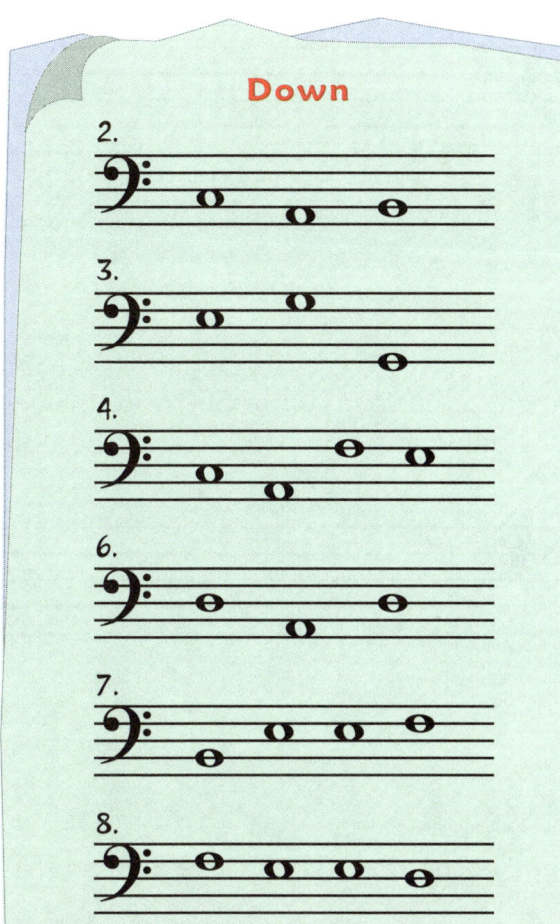

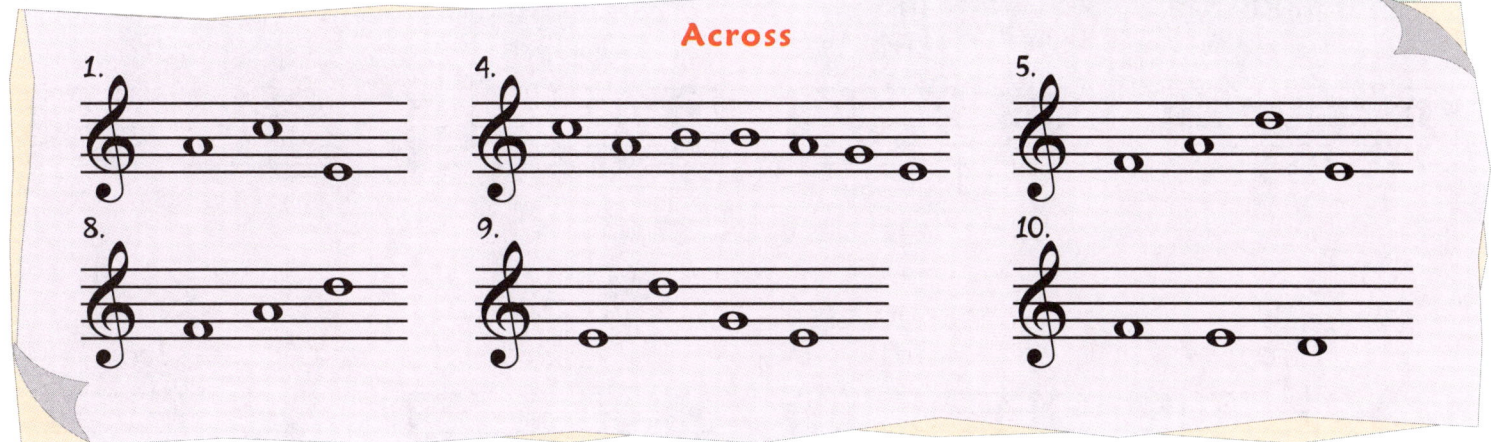

2. Name this note.  How many times is it used in the bass clef words above? _____

3. Name this note.  How many times is it used in the bass clef words above? _____

28

G 5-Finger Pattern in Bass Clef

1. Using semibreves, write the G 5-finger pattern *going up.* Name each note.

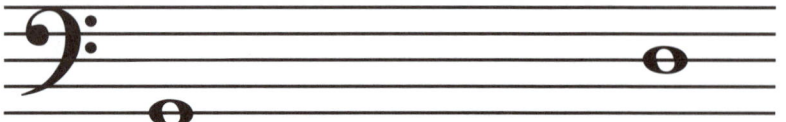

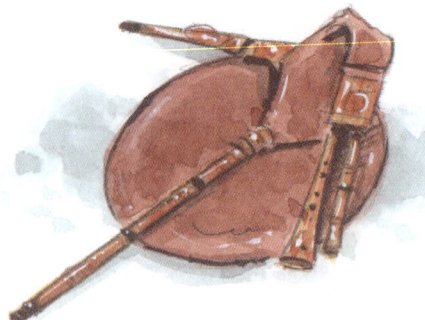

2. Using a semibreve, write one note that will make a 3rd between each note. Name the notes.

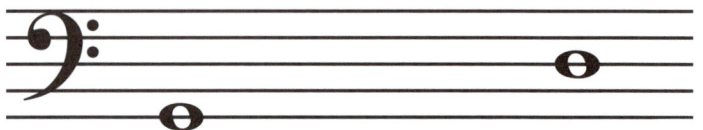

Learning Link

The **musette** is a French dance that was popular during Johann Sebastian Bach's time. Most musettes have repeated notes in the bass, imitating a musical instrument that was much like a bagpipe. Bach wrote several musettes that are still popular and played by students today.

3. Name each note. Then circle *2nd* or *3rd.*

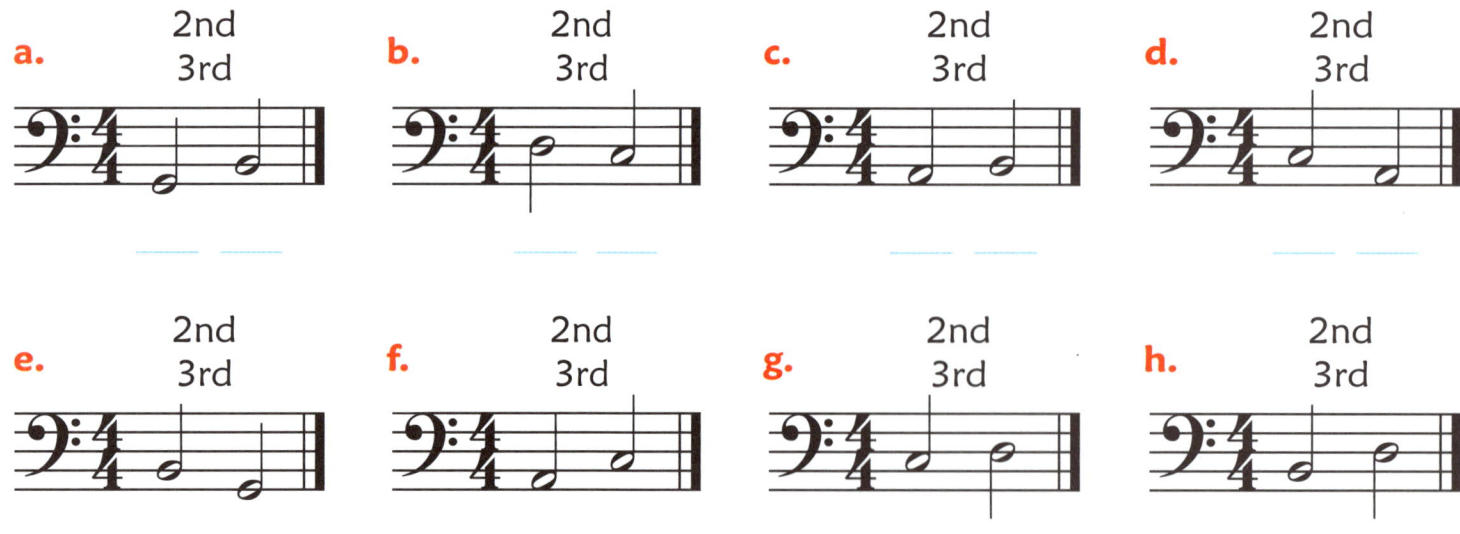

Imagination Station

Press and hold down the sustain pedal to create the sound of bells. Slowly play Low G, then up a 3rd; Bass G, up a 3rd; Treble G, up a 3rd. First play f; then repeat p.

1. **Now Hear This:** Circle the rhythm that your teacher taps or claps.*

a.

b.

Learning Link

The **yo-yo** is one of the oldest toys in history. It can be traced to ancient Greece and China. The word yo-yo comes from the Philippine language and means "come back." Donald F. Duncan, Sr. first promoted the yo-yo in the United States beginning in 1929. Its popularity has risen and fallen throughout the years just like the yo-yo itself. In 1985 the yo-yo was one of the first toys taken into space on the space shuttle Discovery.

2. **Now Play This:** Play and count aloud.

*****Note to Teacher:** Tap or clap one pattern from each exercise.

4ths

1. Write the musical alphabet letter that is *up* a 4th.

a. D   A ^{x x}

b. C ^{x x}

c. G ^{x x}

d. D ^x

2. Write the musical alphabet letter that is *down* a 4th.

a. E _{x x}

b. A _{x x}

c. F _{x x}

d. C _{x x}

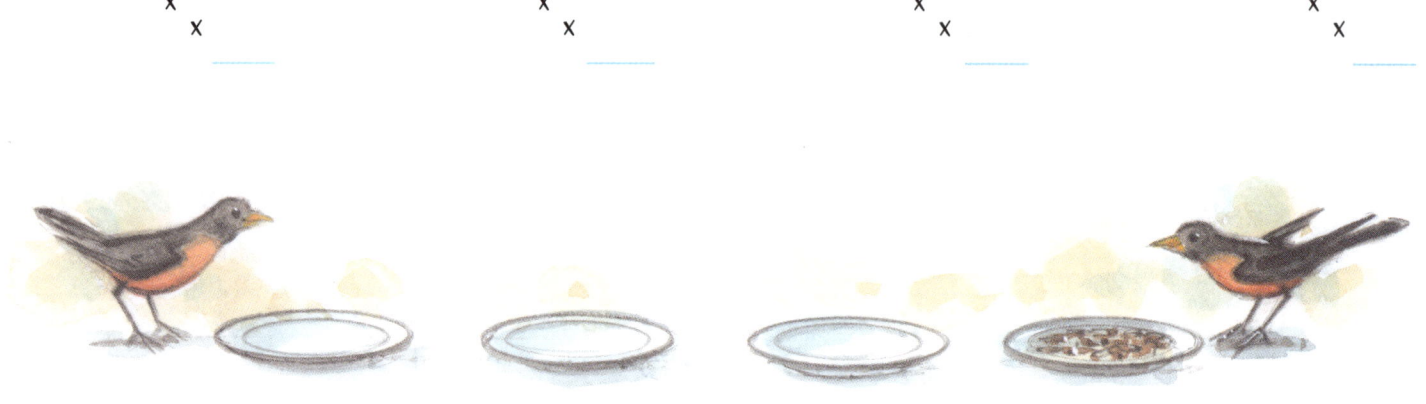

3. Draw a ✓ under all the 4ths on the staves and keyboards.
Write the name of the interval under the others.

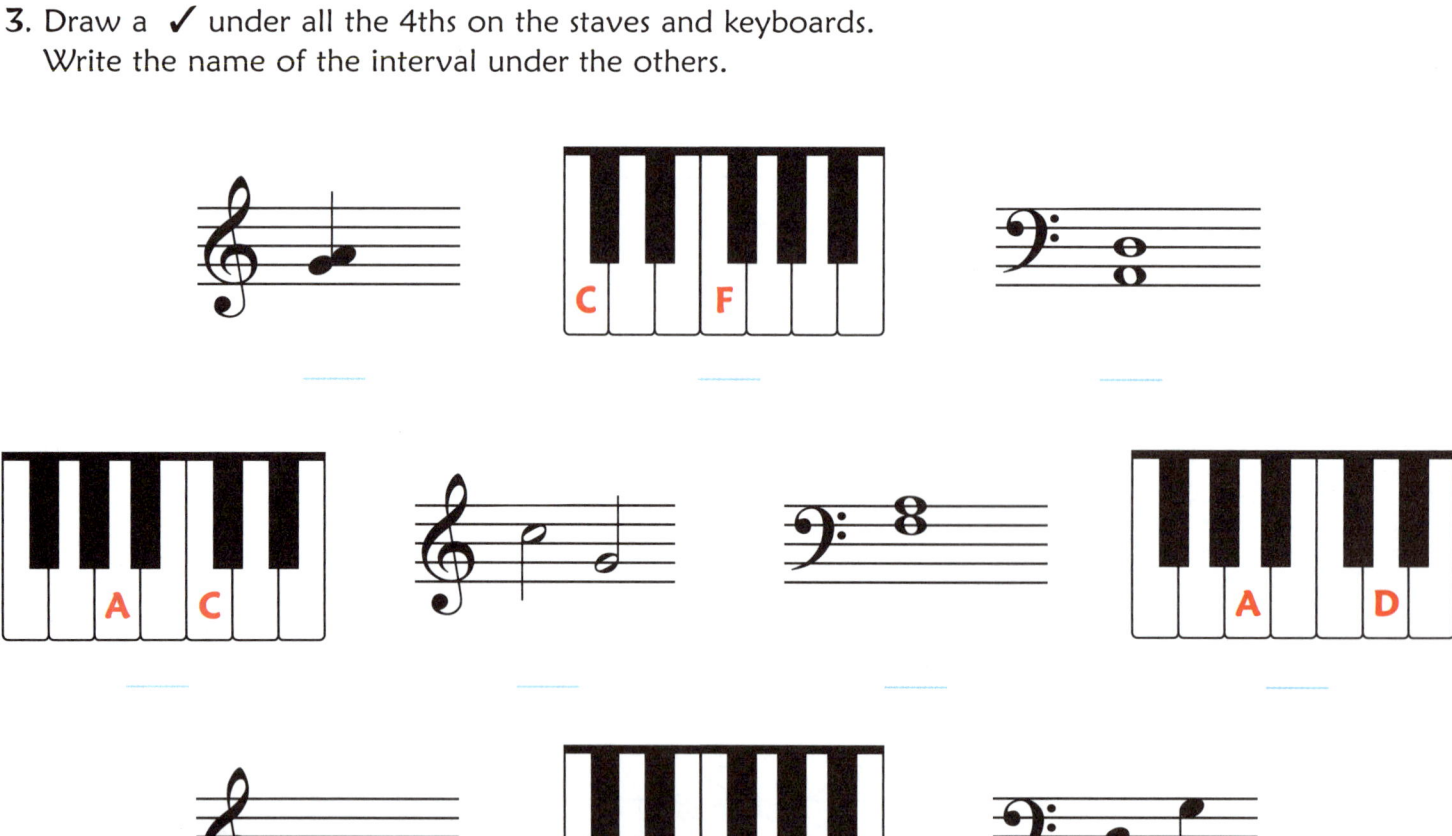

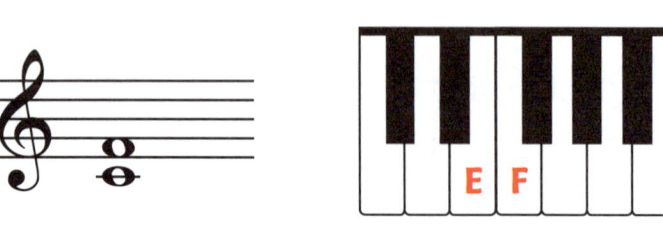

Fun Zone Review

Think of each question as a puzzle piece.
Fill in the blanks and draw the missing semibreves.

1. G 5-Finger Pattern

Learning Link

Jigsaw puzzles were first made by European mapmakers in the 1760s. They pasted maps onto wood and cut them into small pieces with a jigsaw. The "map puzzles" have been a successful educational toy since then to teach geography to children. In the early 1900s, puzzles became very popular with adults as well, and are enjoyed today by all ages. Because wood puzzles are so expensive, most puzzles now are made of cardboard.

2. Draw a melodic 4th *up.*

3. Musical Sentence: ⊓

4. Harmonic ____

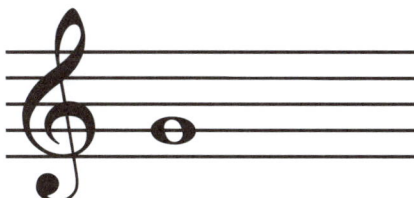

5. One octave higher: ___ va

6. **Ritardando (rit.):**

gradually _____ down the tempo

7. Draw a melodic 3rd *down.*

8. Harmonic ____

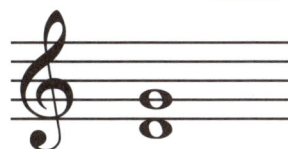

5ths

1. Write the musical alphabet letter that is *up* a 5th.

a.    **b.**    **c.**    **d.**

2. Write the musical alphabet letter that is *down* a 5th.

a. D 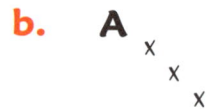   **b.** A    **c.** B    **d.** F

3. Draw a ✓ under all the 5ths on the staves and keyboards.
Write the name of the interval under the others.

   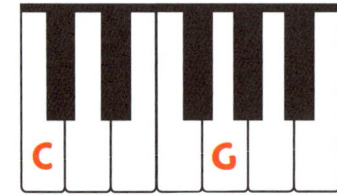   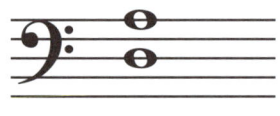

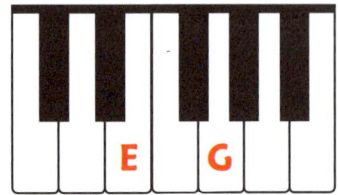         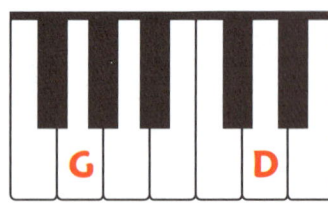

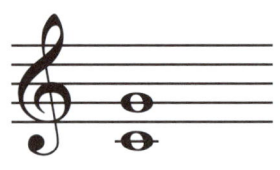   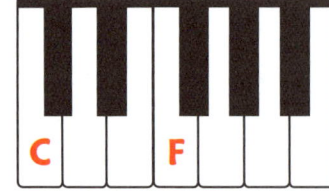   

4ths and 5ths

1. Circle *4th* or *5th* to identify the interval.

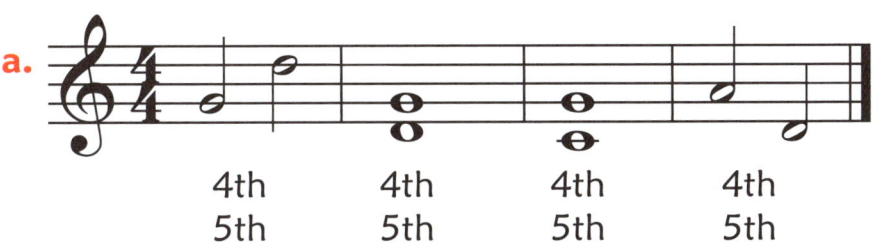

| 4th | 4th | 4th | 4th |
| 5th | 5th | 5th | 5th |

| 4th | 4th | 4th | 4th |
| 5th | 5th | 5th | 5th |

Learning Link

The many sounds of **bells** *are an important part of daily life. They come in all shapes and sizes. Bells were first developed in Asia and were known to exist in ancient China. China's most famous bell, dating from 1415, is found in Beijing and weighs about 60 tons. Other famous bells are* Big Ben *in London and the* Liberty Bell *in Philadelphia.*

2. Circle the 4ths in the music. Then play and count aloud.

mf

How many 4ths did you circle? _____

3. Circle the 5ths in the music. Then play and count aloud.

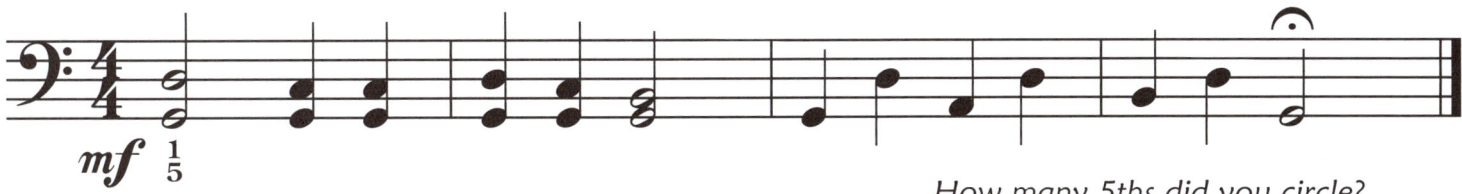

mf

How many 5ths did you circle? _____

4. Write the interval name on the line. Then circle H for harmonic or M for melodic.

H   M   H   M   H   M   H   M   H   M

H   M   H   M   H   M   H   M   H   M

Semitones Up

1. Draw an X on the key that is a *semitone higher* than the named key.

a.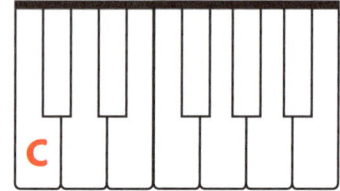

b.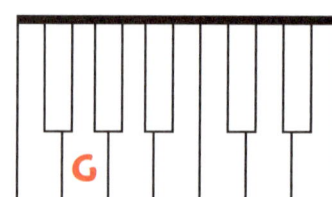

c.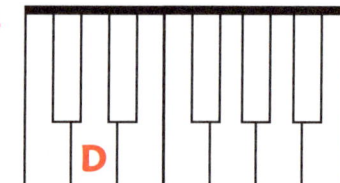

d.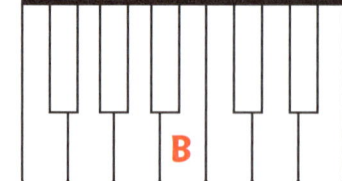

e.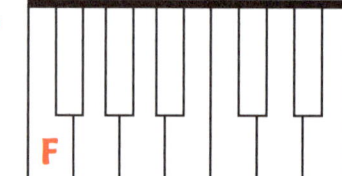

f.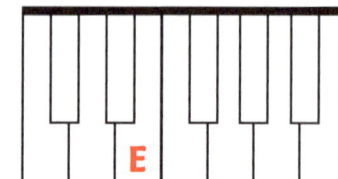

Sharp Sign

2. Connect each note to its correct keyboard.
Below each keyboard, write the name of the sharp.

 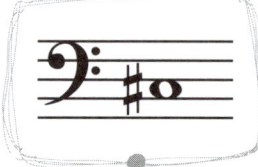   

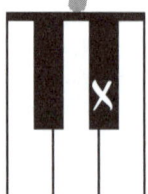    

More About Sharps

The inside square of each sharp is *on* a line or *in* a space.

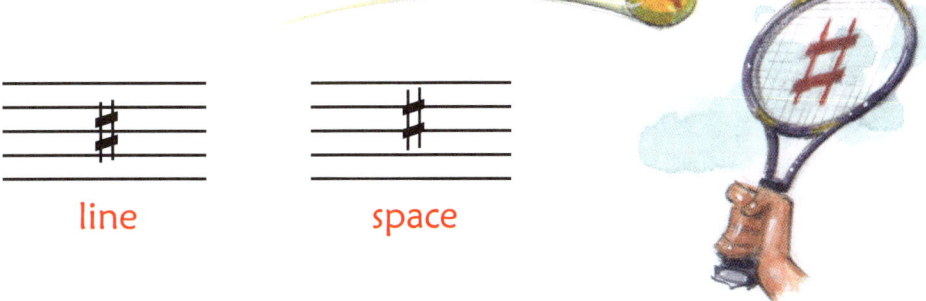

line   space

1. Trace the sharp on line 1. Then draw sharps *on* the other lines.

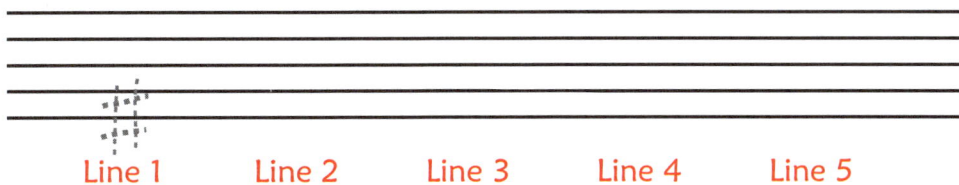

Line 1   Line 2   Line 3   Line 4   Line 5

2. Trace the sharp in space 1. Then draw sharps *in* the other spaces.

Space 1   Space 2   Space 3   Space 4

3. Draw a sharp in front of each note. Then write the name of the note.

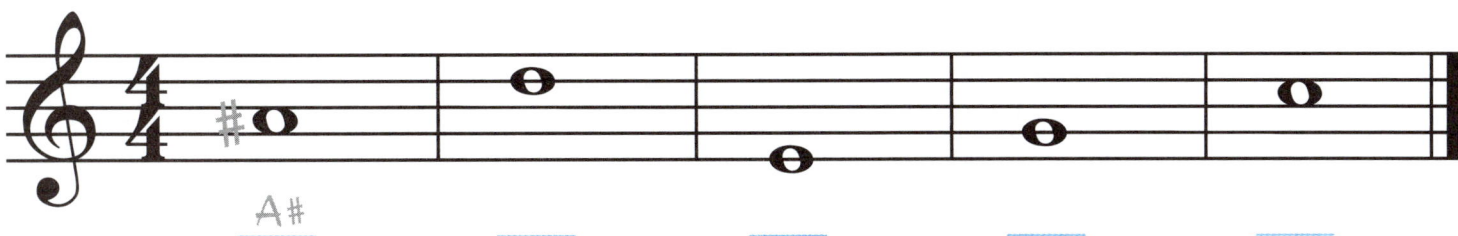

A♯

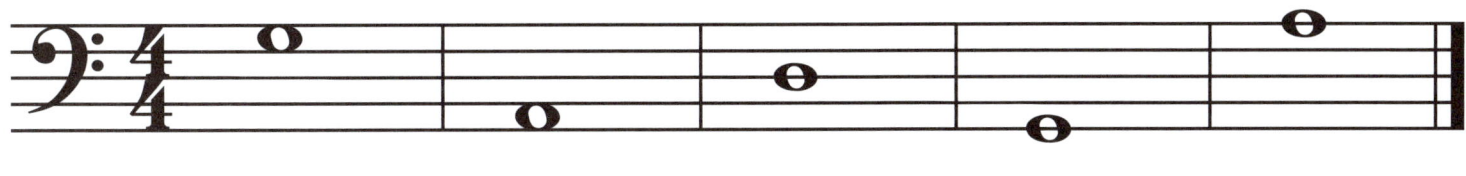

4. **Now Play This:** Play each note pattern. Then write the name of the last note.

LH   3rd   4th   5th

RH   2nd   4th   5th

Fun Zone **Musical Detective**

A sharp applies to the same note for the rest of the bar. It must be written again for each new bar.

1. Be a musical detective by answering the questions about the music. Then play and count aloud.

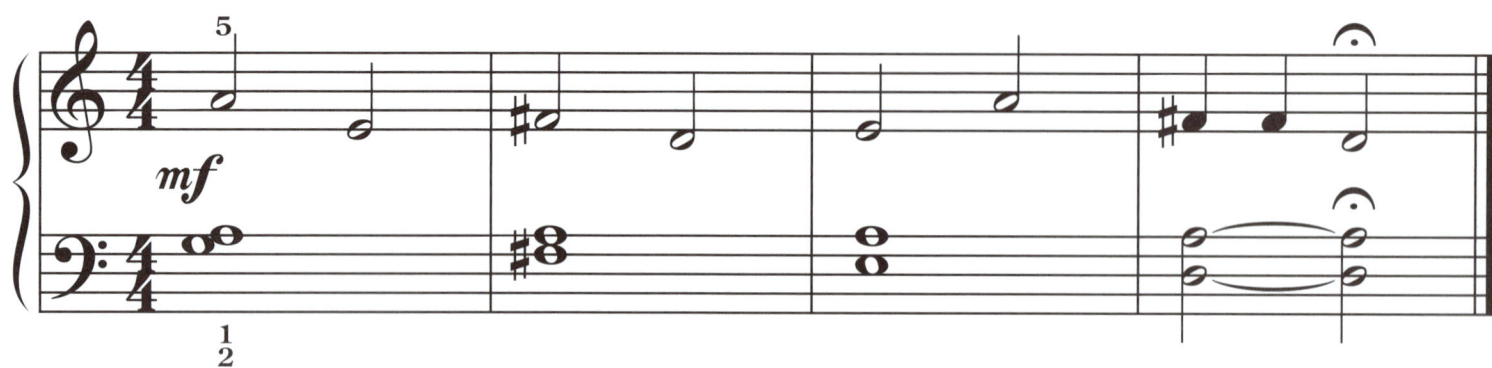

a. Does the RH of bar 1 have a melodic 4th or 5th? _____

b. Does the LH of bar 4 have a harmonic 4th or 5th? _____

c. Which bar has a fermata? _____

d. In the RH of bar 4, how many notes are played as sharps? _____

2. **Now Play This:** Play and count aloud. Below each bar, write the number of times that you played a sharp in that bar.

a.

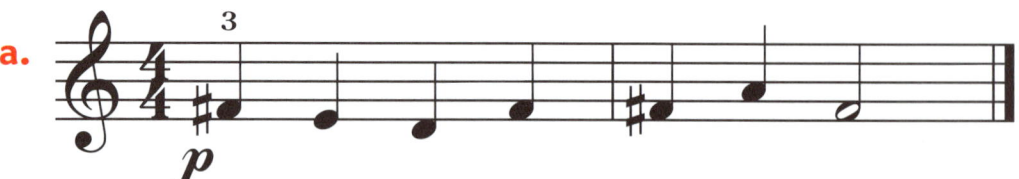

b.

Incomplete Bars

1. Circle the incomplete bars. Write the counts under each exercise. Then clap and count aloud.

a.

b.

c.

Learning Link

In 1914, the United States Congress made **Mother's Day** *a national day of celebration. Mothers are honoured by families on the second Sunday in May. This celebration probably comes from an old English tradition of honouring mothers,* called Mothering Sunday.

2. **Now Hear This:** Your teacher will play the written note and then a note *up* or *down* a 4th.*
Using a minim, write the second note.
Remember: *Stems* down *if notehead is* on *line 3 or above.*
Stems up *if notehead is* below *line 3.*

a.    **b.**    **c.**

Imagination Station

Select the notes in example ***a*** *or* ***b*** *to complete the melody, and write them in the music. Then play and count aloud.*

a.    **b.**

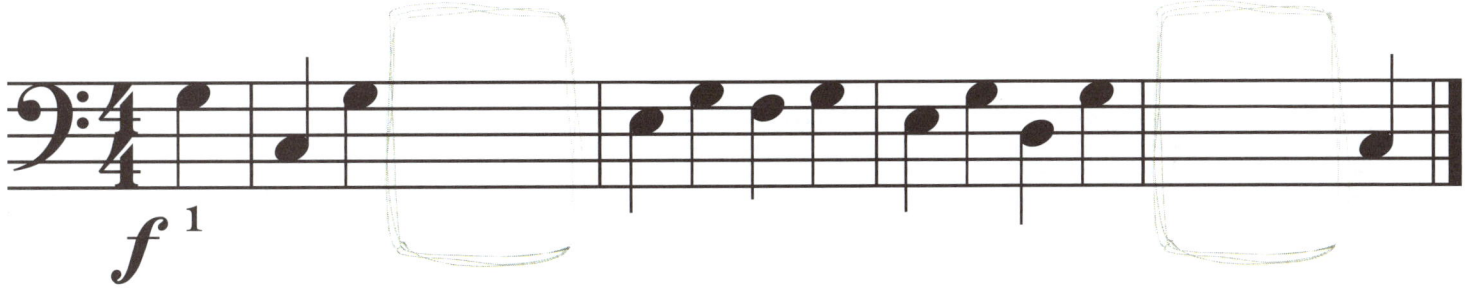

*****Note to Teacher:** In the middle of the keyboard, play the given note and then a 4th up or down.

38

New Rhythm Pattern

Lesson Book: page 38

1. In the blank bars, write the new rhythm using the note that is *up a 4th* from Bass G.

New Rhythm on Bass G

Name
note _____

2. Complete the new rhythm on D.

3. Write the new rhythm using the note that is *down a 4th* from D.

Name
note _____

3. **Now Play This:** Play and count aloud.

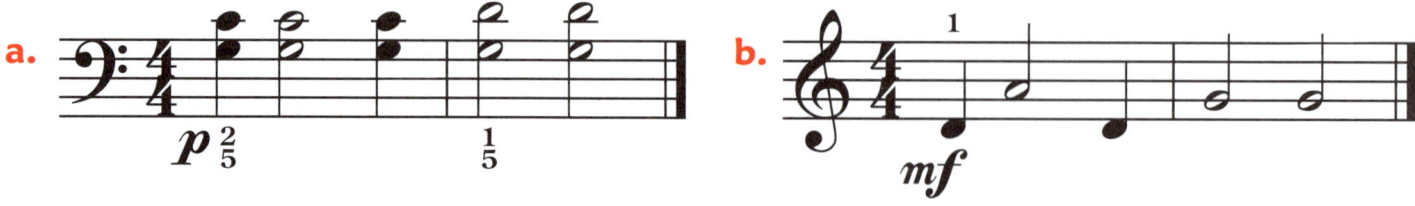

4. **Now Hear This:** Your teacher will play the written note and then a note *up* or *down* a 5th.*
Using a minim, write the second note.
Remember: Stems *down* if notehead is *on* line 3 or above.
Stems *up* if notehead is *below* line 3.

*****Note to Teacher:** In the middle of the keyboard, play the given note and then a 5th up or down.

Fun Zone **Baseball Intervals**

Name each interval to find out how many hits each player made in today's game. Score a home run by answering all correctly.

Centre fielder

Example: 4

Left fielder

Second baseman

Right fielder

Third baseman

First baseman

Pitcher

Catcher

Batter

Home run hit by

_____
Your Name

Rhythm and Interval Review

1. Draw an X through one note or rest in each bar
   so that it has the correct number of beats.

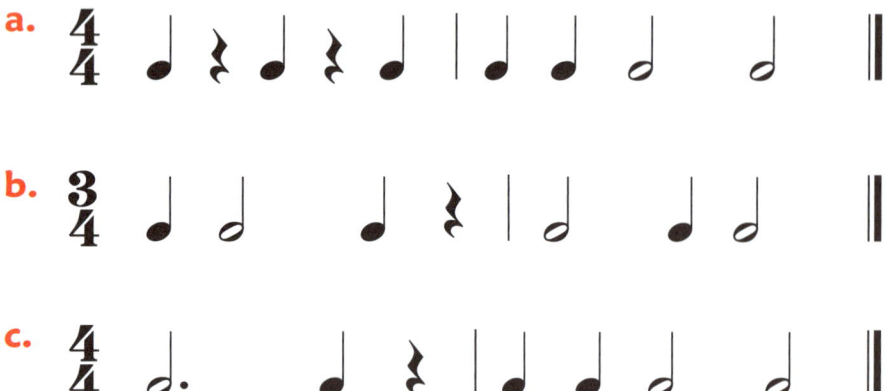

2. Using a crotchet, write each melodic interval *up* and *down* from Treble G.
   Remember: Stems *down* if notehead is *on* line 3 or above.
   Stems *up* if notehead is *below* line 3.

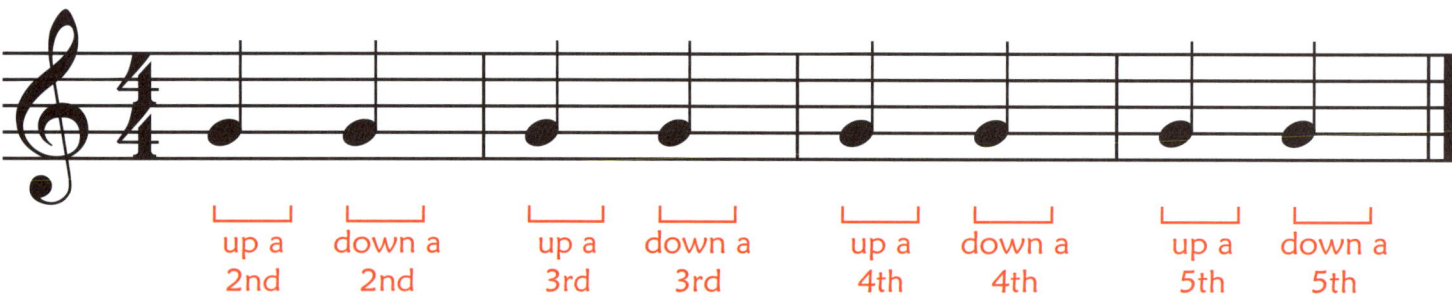

3. Draw a line to connect each sign to its meaning.

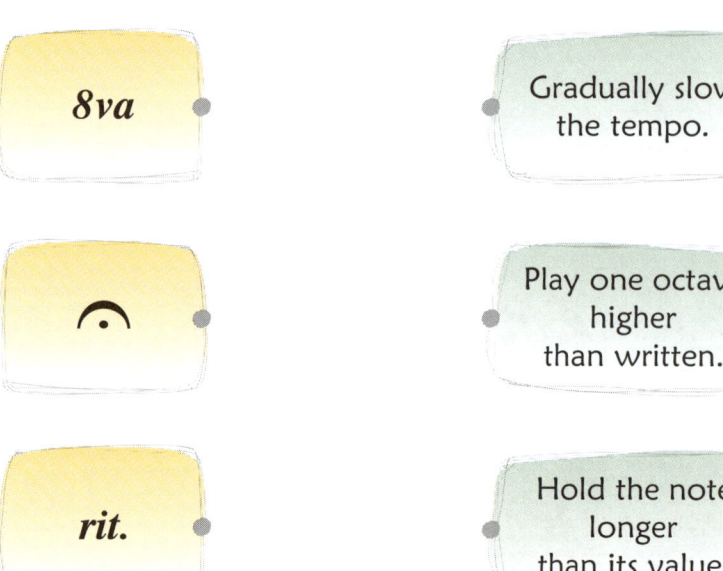

8va	Gradually slow the tempo.
⌢	Play one octave higher than written.
rit.	Hold the note longer than its value.

1. **Now Hear This:** Your teacher will play a *2nd* or *4th.**
   Circle the interval that you hear.

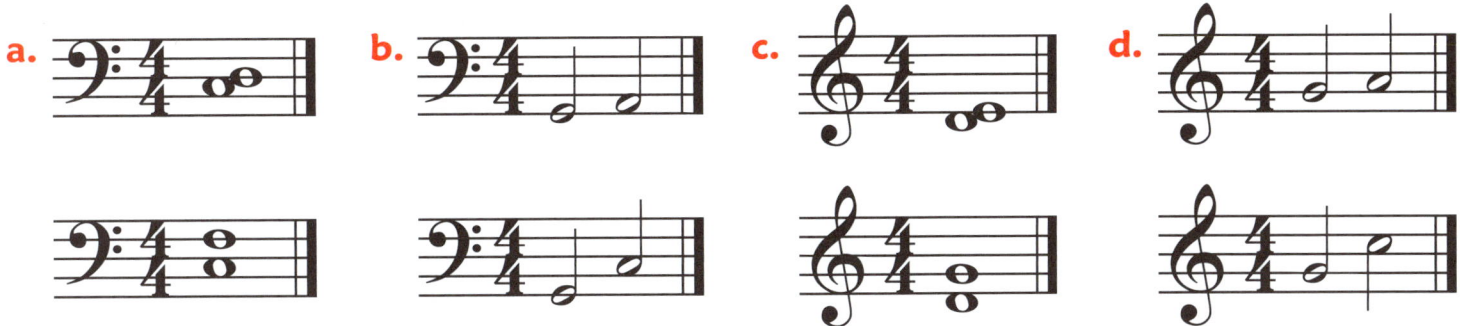

2. **Now Play This:** Play and count aloud.

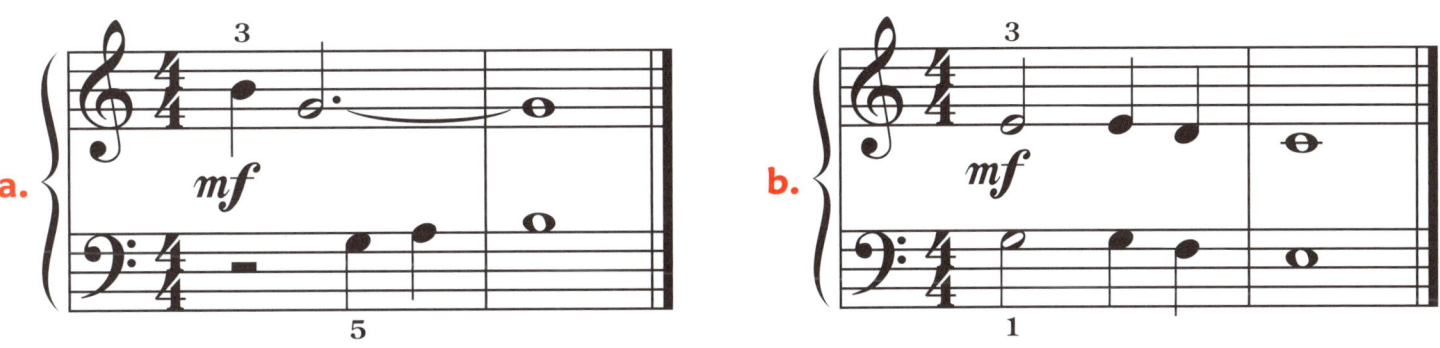

🪐 *Imagination Station*

Using the rhythm above the stave, play your own
RH melody using melodic 2nds, 3rds, 4ths or 5ths.
Start on G with finger 1.
Optional: Write your favourite melody on the stave.

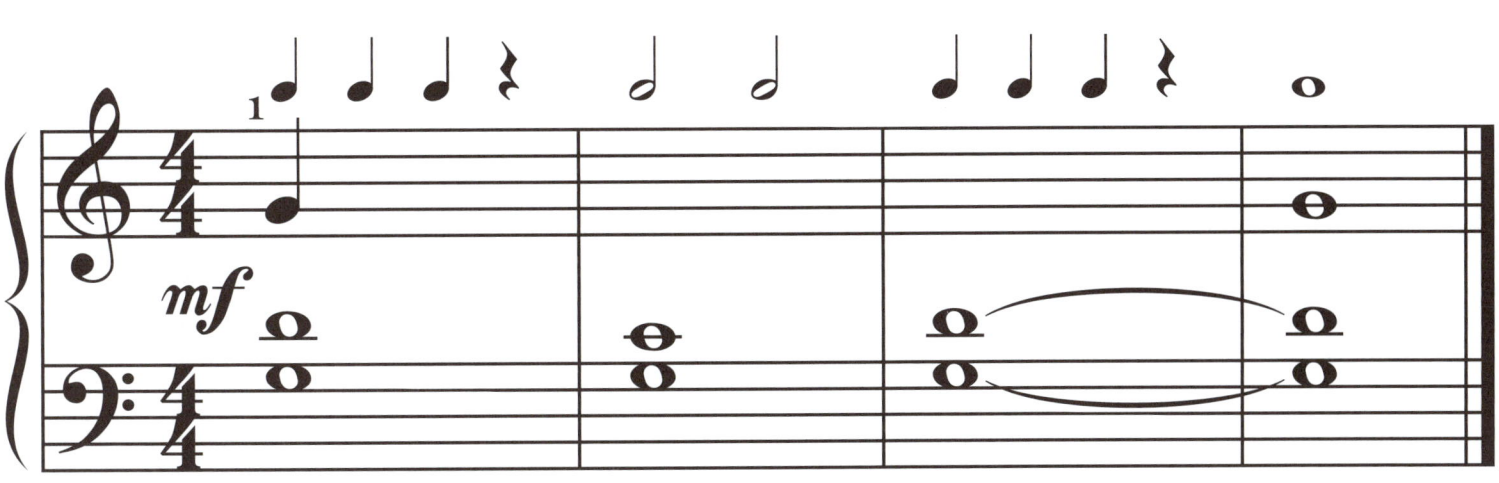

***Note to Teacher:** Play one interval from each exercise.

Semitones Down

1. Draw an X on the key that is a *semitone lower* than the named key.

a.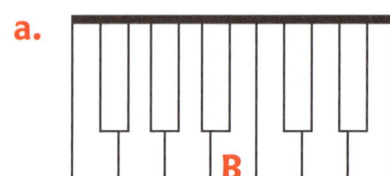

b.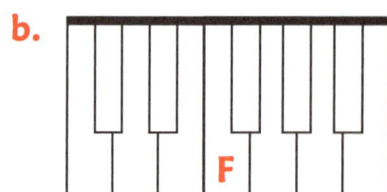

c.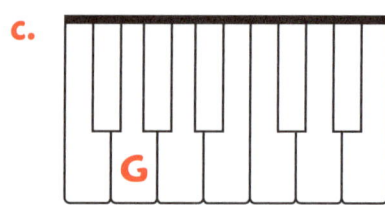

d.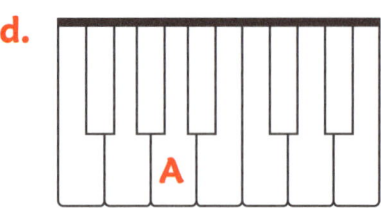

e.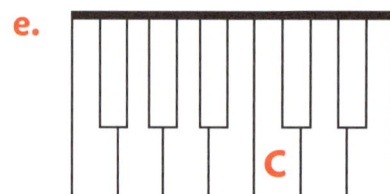

f.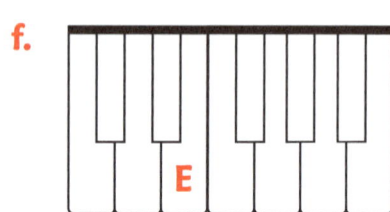

Flat Sign

2. Connect each note to its correct keyboard.
Below each keyboard, write the name of the flat.

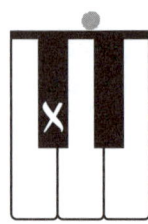

More About Flats

The round part of each flat is *on* a line or *in* a space.

line   space

1. Trace the flat on line 1. Then draw flats *on* the other lines.

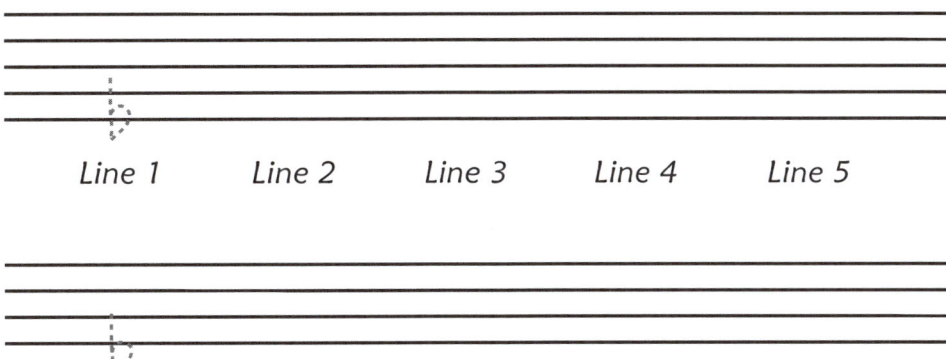

Line 1   Line 2   Line 3   Line 4   Line 5

2. Trace the flat in space 1. Then draw flats *in* the other spaces.

Space 1   Space 2   Space 3   Space 4

3. Draw a flat in front of each note. Then write the name of the note.

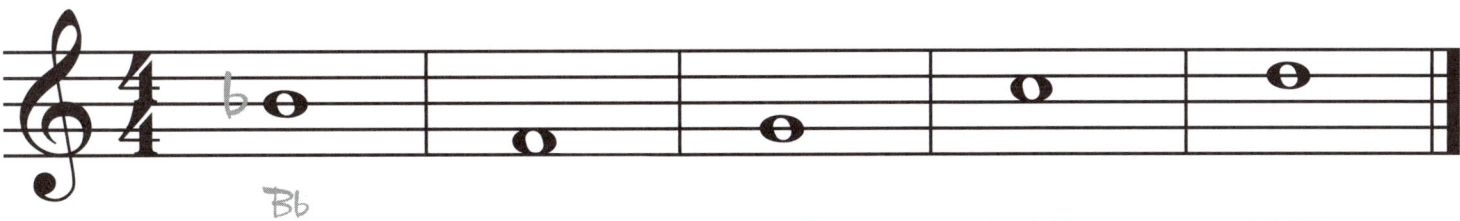

Bb _____ _____ _____ _____

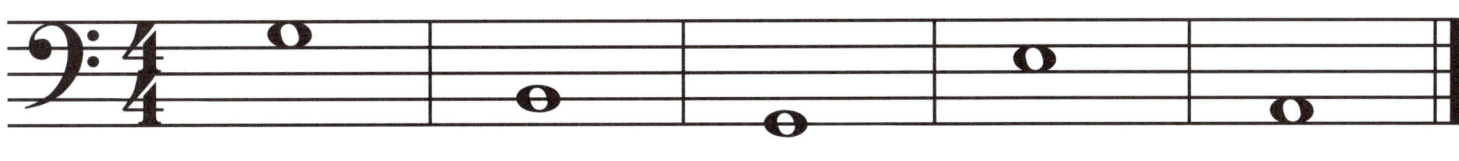

_____ _____ _____ _____ _____

4. **Now Play This:** Play each note pattern. Then write the name of the last note.

a. LH

5th   3rd   3rd   2nd

b. RH

3rd   3rd   4th   2nd

Fun Zone Musical Detective

A flat applies to the same note for the rest of the bar. It must be written again for each new bar.

1. Be a musical detective by answering the questions about the music. Then play and count aloud.

a. How many times is B played as a flat in bar 1? _____

b. What harmonic interval is found in the LH? _____

c. Which hand moves up an octave? _____

d. In what bar does the music begin to slow down gradually? _____

e. Does the RH play melodic or harmonic intervals? _____

2. **Now Play This:** Play and count aloud. Below each bar, write the number of times that you played a flat in that bar.

a.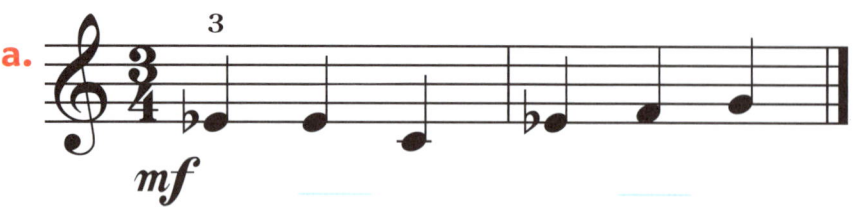

b.

Learning Link

*Every day thousands of children go to school with **lunch boxes** decorated with pictures of celebrities, cartoon characters or popular images of the time. The lunch box as we know it today began around 1950 when the Hopalong Cassidy lunch box was invented. It was based on the popular TV show of the same name. Since that time, television has continued to influence the pictures on lunch boxes.*

Fun Zone **Visit the Pyramids**

Play each example as you follow
the desert trail up to the pyramids.

6. Play.

Lift hand—
don't stretch

5. Play a RH harmonic 5th
with finger 1 on Middle C.

4. Play.

3. Play.

2. Play Treble G with RH finger 2,
then play up a semitone.

1. Play on Bass G.

Begin Here

1. **Now Hear This:** Your teacher will play a *3rd* or *5th.**
   Circle the interval that you hear.

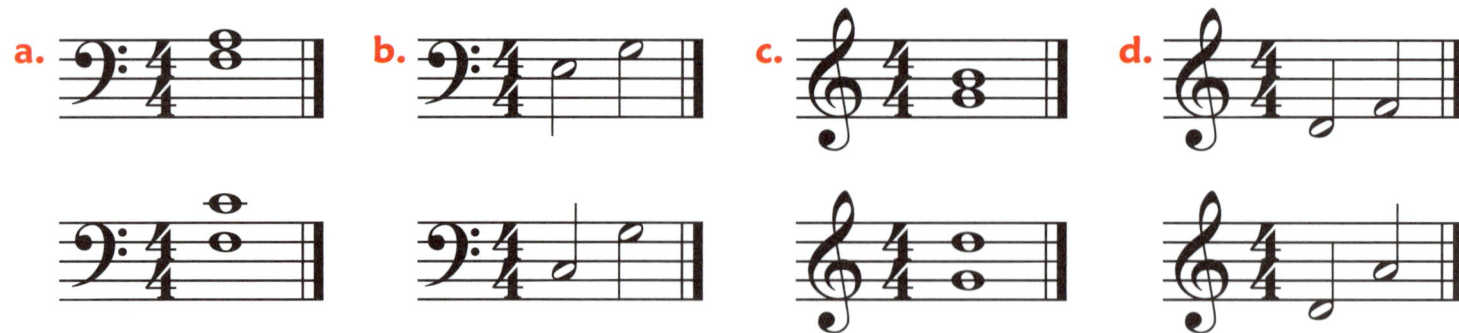

Imagination Station

Complete *Faraway Drums* by adding:
- • a dynamic sign at the beginning
- • a **rit.** near the end
- • an **8va**
- • a flat before each B
- • a fermata on the last notes

Then play.

Faraway Drums

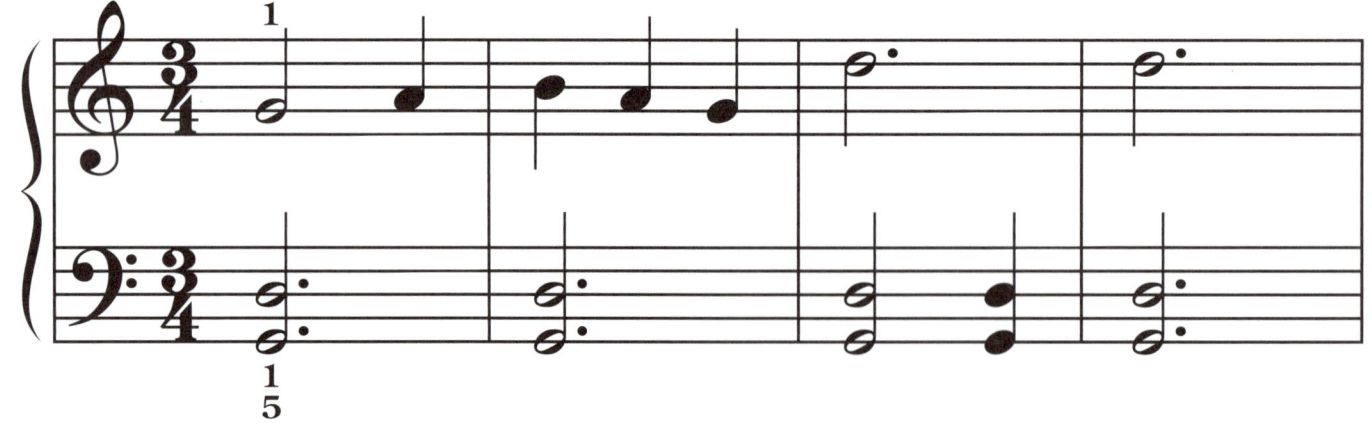

*Note to Teacher:** Play one interval from each exercise.

Fun Zone Landmark Tour Bus

Name each landmark note you see
on your tour up through the big city.

5.

State's Tallest Building

4.

Magic Music Theatre

6.

Premier Concert Hall

Fabulous Fun Amusement Park

2.

Sunrise Baseball Park

3.

1.

Gorgeous Gardens

$\mathcal{B}$egin Here

Landmark Tours
See famous landmarks!

48

Premier Music Review

1. **Now Hear This:** Your teacher will play the first note and then a semitone *up* or *down*.*
   - Draw a sharp sign before the second note if it goes *up*.
   - Draw a flat sign before the second note if it goes *down*.

a.    b.    c.

d.    e. 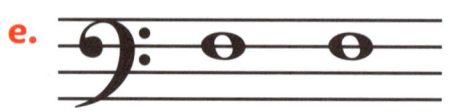   f.

2. Name the notes.

 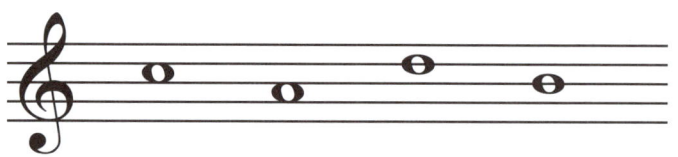

3. Using a crotchet, write each melodic interval *up* and *down* from Bass G.
   Remember: Stems *down* if notehead is *on* line 3 or above.
   Stems *up* if notehead is *below* line 3.

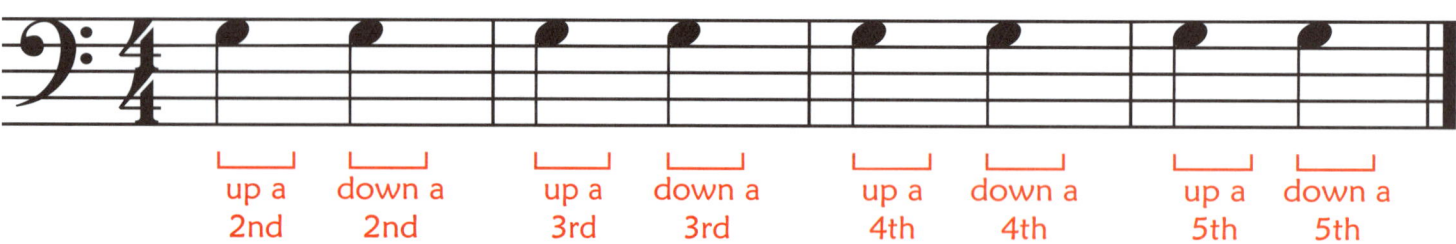

4. Write the counts below each rhythm. Then tap and count aloud.

***Note to Teacher:** Play the first note of exercise and then a semitone *up* or *down*.